Endorser

Marriage is God's brainchild. He dreamt about it, designed it, and established it. He laid down in His infallible word the tenets that are to guide, shape, and strengthen its very existence.

It's no wonder then that the arch-enemy of our souls would rally every available force in the kingdom of darkness against this chief institution, in an attempt to destroy it and completely obliterate it from its place of honour and esteem.

This book is a timely resource in helping you address and resolve many of the questions and situations that you will encounter in your journey into and through marriage, from bedroom intimacy to raising children, from finances to forgiveness. It tackles real issues to ensure your marriage is built to last.

Having known Jennifer for many years and seeing her walk her talk, it is our deep pleasure and conviction to highly recommend and endorse this wonderful book. Written in an easy-to-read, practical, and down-to-earth style, you will find it at once delightful, insightful, and refreshing.

Come and join us as we embark on this amazing journey through corridors of knowledge and highways of personal experience, and into wells of wisdom.

Consider yourself warned:
+ You will be blessed.
+ You will be challenged.
+ You will be transformed.
+ You will be inspired.

Happy reading!

Bishop Allan and Reverend Kathy Kiuna
Jubilee Christian Church, Nairobi, Kenya

Jennifer has openly shared her experiences in a simple, yet profound and compelling manner. 'Marriage Built to last' is an easy read, the kind of book one could easily relate with and tell one's self that 'if she could make it, so can I'. The theme of the book is captured in its title and that comes out in a very strong way throughout the book. Marriage is built to last, if it is built on Christ, the solid Rock'.

In 'Marriage built to last', Jennifer deals, in a very practical and Christ-centered way, with issues such as communication in marriage, intimacy, sex, infidelity, and finances. An additional topic involves relationships with extended families, particularly mothers-in-law.

The author is convinced that Christ is the 'foundation' of marriages, the builder of marriages and the 'Pillar' who holds marriages together. In a nut-shell Christ intends for marriages to last. Marriages may have their challenges but she believes that success in marriage is based on the couple's level of commitment, patience, and sacrifice, which is what counts in any relationship.

'Marriage built to Last' is not only for married couples but also for those aspiring to get married. As you read this book, may your ideas be transformed; for singles, may you have a clearer perspective of marriage and for the married, may the cords of love among you and your spouse be strengthened, restored and rebuilt so that you too can help someone along the way.

Marionne Tucker
Author: Marriage on The Rock
Founder & President of His Glory Revealed Ministries
Garnet Valley, PA, USA

In this book, Jennifer fuses her faith in God, her personal journey of life and family, her counseling skills, her knowledge of God's ideal in His Word and her passion for a happy, fulfilling and meaningful marriage life. The book is filled with godly principles and practical ideas to help any one wanting to get married and at the same time bring renewal and refreshment to those already married.

Rev. Elijah Wanje,
Senior Pastor, Ridgeways Baptist Church, Nairobi, Kenya

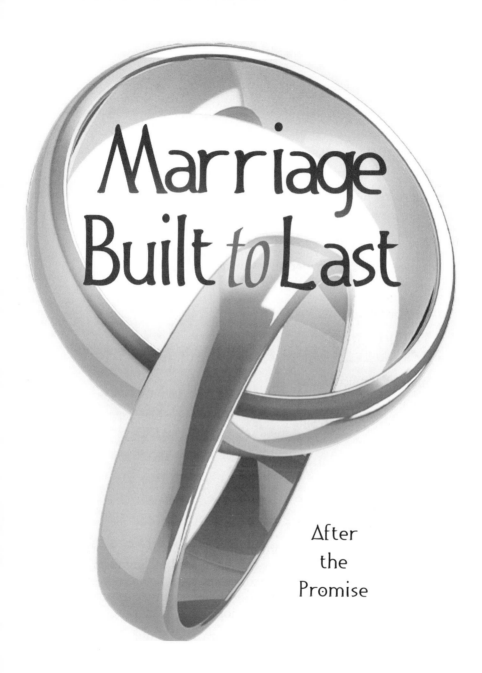

Marriage Built *to* Last

After
the
Promise

Jennifer Karina
Nairobi

Marriage Built to Last

Copyright © 2011 by Jennifer Karina

Published by:

Integrity Publishers Inc.

P.O. Box 789,

Wake Forest, NC 27588

U.S.A.

info@integritypublishers.org

ISBN 13: 978-0-9828630-9-1

Unless otherwise indicated, Scripture quotations are from *The New International Version*. ®. Copyright © 1973, 1978, 1984 International Bible Society. All italics, bold print, etc., are for the author's emphasis.

Printed in Kenya by English Press Ltd

Contents

Foreword vii
Preface ix
Acknowledgements xiii

Chapter One
The Big Decision 1

Chapter Two
Successful Courtship 13

Chapter Three
This Is Not the Man I Married! 29

Chapter Four
Managing Attitudes, Self-Esteem, and Confidence 53

Chapter Five
Intimacy and the Marriage Bed 65

Chapter Six
Marriage as God Intended: The Biblical Basis of Marriage .. 89

Chapter Seven
Financial Management in Marriage 101

Chapter Eight
Raising Up Children 121

Chapter Nine
Coping With the Other Woman in His Life 148

Chapter Ten
Marriage and Friendship 158

Bibliography 171

foreword

It is a great honour for me to write the foreword to the first of my wife's many books. I do it gladly and with a deep sense of pride. Jennie has been my wife and business partner for many years now. Without her love, encouragement, and support, I could not have attained the success I enjoy today. She is my pillar of strength.

When I first met Jennie many years ago, all I saw was her striking physical beauty, which earned her the nickname, "BB" (Black Beauty). She has the greatest pair of legs I have ever set my eyes on—and a fantastic figure to match! As our relationship developed and I came to know her better, however, I realised that she was not just endowed with external beauty. Even more captivating is her beauty within. She is sensitive, kind, generous, considerate, dependable, independent, charismatic, and extremely energetic—always determined to be a winner! Jennie and I have bonded over the years and I have no hesitation in calling her my best friend and soulmate.

Inasmuch as we have enjoyed our marriage over the years, like all couples, we have had our disagreements and challenges. On every occasion, though, we choose to deal with and resolve each one of them. We never go to bed with unresolved issues. I would say our greatest strength has been our openness towards each other. We have continually learnt from our mistakes and benefited from them. As we matured, we have also learnt not to belittle our weaknesses but to focus on each other's strengths, always allowing room for growth.

Jennie married me when I was 25 years of age. I did not know much and did not have much, but she loved me anyway. Together, we have been blessed with three children and, recently, with two grandchilden. We have also 'acquired' three other children: two sons and a daughter. I greatly enjoy being Jennie's husband; I'm grateful to God for her and the children she has given me.

Jennie is not just a great wife and friend; she is also a gifted person who makes the most of everything. I taught her to play golf and she learnt well! Many people wonder how I can play with her, when she beats me—her teacher—at the game! I do not see it that way. For me, whenever she wins, she makes me a winner. It is that simple! I am proud of whatever she does and excels in.

My wife loves to mentor and develop other people. She is a believer in empowering not only others but also herself. That passion has led her to write this book on marriage. She has put everything into our own marital relationship to make it work. I am one happy beneficiary of her vision and determination to see every marriage joyful and fulfilled. I can confidently say that she knows what she talks about. You will be exceedingly enriched by reading it.

Bob Karina
June 2011

Preface

When I first thought of writing this book, many questions rushed through my mind. Several books have already been written about marriage; did we need another book on the subject? What was there to say about it that had not already been said? Other than being a wife for over 30 years, what qualified me to talk to others about marriage?

After much prayer, I realised that my many years of a fulfilling marriage were the very reason I needed to write this book. In the course of our relationship, my husband and I have gone through most of the challenges that break up marriages today—the very ones you may be going through right now. We have come through each experience and used them to strengthen our bond. As a result, my faith in the institution is more affirmed. I believe that it should and, indeed, could work! I needed to share that conviction with some young woman somewhere.

As I deliberated over who should write the foreword for the book, I first considered my mentors; then, my husband Bob offered to write it himself. I was glad that he did because he is the most suitable person to do so, having walked the journey with me. He is part of the voyage and a key player in writing this book. He has been supportive every step of the way; he encouraged me to finish it, so that you may read it and be confident in your own marriage. Whenever I became disheartened, he cheered me on by saying, "Keep going, Jennie! You will be a blessing to someone."

In this book, I have chosen to address my thoughts to the young woman who desires a fulfilling marriage. She may be married already or about to take the life-changing step. My goal is to take her by the hand and lead her down the path I have walked myself. I want to show her that God's intention is to make marriage work and that He provides all that is necessary for it to do so.

My own marriage started with a simple decision. I determined from the onset that my marriage should work no matter what. It has been full of surprises, much joy, and, yes, various challenges. Because of my husband's and my total commitment to the cause, however, today we can look back and enjoy the fruits of our labour.

Over time, I have had the privilege of hosting and facilitating several marriage fitness seminars, women's fellowships, and bridal showers. In all of them, I have noticed that questions and comments that arise almost always revolve around the same issues: communication in marriage, intimacy, sex, infidelity, and finances. An additional topic involves relationships with extended families, particularly mothers-in-law. In these events, the heartbreak moment for me comes when individuals talk to me privately afterwards, concerning their relationship issues. My heart bleeds for them, as I listen to their sad stories. The following narrative is just an example.

A lovely young lady named Joyce has been married for seven years, but she grapples with difficult issues. She was very much in love when she married Paul. Three years after their grand wedding, though, he had lost interest in her and no longer desired her company. He spent a lot of time away from home – sometimes for a whole weekend – without explanation. When he did give a reason, it was usually flimsy: taking the car for repairs or going for a haircut. He would often come home drunk, after being with his boys. He did not care to find out how Joyce felt or how their children were doing. She felt alone, afraid, frustrated, and confused, having no one to confide in or share her pain with.

As things deteriorated, Joyce discovered that her husband was having an affair with her maid of honour: a childhood friend and confidante. And as if that were not enough, he had lost his job but did not disclose it to his wife. He woke up every morning "to go to work", so she never suspected anything. Money did not seem to be a problem; he always provided for his family.

Joyce continued, "I will never forget that cold Saturday morning in June, when I heard a knock on the door. I thought it was my husband, who never carries his house keys, returning from a night out. Angry and frustrated, I opened the door. It was an unexpected visitor. What he had with him changed my life forever. Apparently, my husband had taken out a loan without my knowledge, with our home as collateral. Because he had failed to keep up with the repayments, our house had been auctioned. The visitor had come to serve us with an eviction notice; the new owner needed to move in. I could not believe this was happening to me!"

This book is a response to these stories of despair – told and untold – like Joyce's. Using biblical principles, I have done my best to answer many questions about marriage. I do this in obedience to God's word in Titus 2:3-5, which says:

Likewise, teach the older women to be reverent in the way they live, not to be slanderers or addicted to much wine, but to teach what is good. Then they can urge the younger women to love their husbands and children, to be self-controlled and pure, to be busy at home, to be kind, and to be subject to their husbands, so that no one will malign the word of God.

I sincerely hope that this book will enrich your relationship and that you will enjoy greater love and unity with your loved one, as God intended for you. May you be inspired, encouraged, empowered, and never be the same again! Read on.

Jennifer Karina
June 2011

Acknowledgements

First, to the Almighty God. Because of Him, all things are possible. This book is a testimony of God's faithfulness.

To Bob, my beloved husband, friend, and soulmate, who has faithfully walked the journey of life with me. Being married to you has been great! A journey of joy, fulfilment, challenge, and adventure! I appreciate your love, commitment, and dedication to me, our children, and the entire family.

To my most precious daughters: Rina, Ciru, and Chidi, and my sons: Roni, Alan, and Bo: You are my pride and crown. Thanks for making parenting such a joy and delight, and for always inspiring me.

To my daughters and sisters in the ministry. Because of you, I have had the passion and enthusiasm to put this book together. Thank you for sharing your lives with me and allowing me the opportunity to mentor you and to walk with you. May your marriages blossom!

To my mentors and friends, who have constantly kept me accountable. Because of you, this book has become a reality. I thank God for each one of you. I appreciate you all for your guidance, love, and friendship.

To Pastors Elijah Wanje and Fred Geke: Your guidance, mentorship, and faith in me made the difference. Thumbs up to you! And to Wambui Gatigwa, thanks for planting the seed in my heart that "...lack of guidance [makes a nation fall], but victory is won through many advisers" (Proverbs 11:14).

Chapter One

The Big Decision

When your values are clear to you,
making decisions become easier.
Roy Disney

Making the marriage decision is straightforward and simple for many people. For others, however, it is not as easy. I have come to learn that people marry for different reasons. Many do so because they feel it is time; others because they desire to start a family. Some tie the knot because the love bug has bitten them, while others want to satisfy their desires. There are even those who marry to escape difficulties at home, while some have confessed to marrying just for an opportunity to live in a foreign land or to be financially stable. Others wed simply to keep up with their friends and peers. During bridal showers, I often ask those present why they got married or want to get married, and it is always interesting to hear some of their responses.

Once married, some people, at one time or another, wonder whether they actually married the right person. Since this question inevitably arises somewhere along the marriage, I cannot overstate the need to make wise decisions in choosing a life partner. Having interacted with several young people seeking for a marriage partner for themselves, I have concluded that many of them have unrealistic expectations, fantasies, and ideas. Many look for perfect combinations that are simply hard to come by. For instance, women set their hearts on meeting and marrying Prince Charming: a handsome man who drives preferably the latest sports car, has a good source of income, and lives in a reputable neighbourhood. Outside the world of dreams and fairy tales, this is hardly possible for everyone.

Is There a Specific Person for Someone?

While some people are in a fantasy world, others believe that God created one and only one person specifically for them to marry. Is there really such a thing as just one special individual designated by God for a person? Does God identify particular life partners for everyone? I cannot find scriptural grounds to support that idea, but I know He gives us the freedom to make our own choices. God has a good plan for our lives—our marriages, too— as long as we are sensitive and obedient to His word.

According to scripture, Mary was engaged to Joseph. Joseph, on the other hand, looked forward to his firstborn child with her, but God had something else in mind for them. Mary conceived through the power of the Holy Spirit and gave birth to the Saviour Jesus Christ. God's plans are not human plans. Although we may be fixated on particular people, the outcome may be different. We need to stay open-minded to them.

Sometime back, I knew a young man who dated a lovely girl. He was sure that she was the one for him. He claimed that the Lord had confirmed this to him on various occasions. One "confirmation" had come through a dream, another through his close friend, and a third through a stranger. He then visited the girl's parents and informed them of his intention to marry their daughter. Sadly, the marriage never happened. During their courtship, he met someone else and, this time, "the Lord spoke in a clearer and louder voice" to say that the new girl was actually the one! To this day, the jilted girl still hurts and has not moved on to find someone else. She is still convinced that he was the man for her. I have no doubt that this same scenario is being reenacted somewhere else, even as I write this.

Having listened to many different couples' stories of meeting each other, I have concluded that there are many potential partners for any one individual. I recently had the privilege of meeting some old friends whom I had not seen for a while. As we talked, I asked them how they had met their spouses. When they shared their stories, I could see their eyes sparkle, as they relived those moments. Some had met in school, while others met in college, church, a neighbourhood, or the workplace. Others were introduced by a mutual friend. One had met her husband on the Internet. Apparently, he had responded to an online dating advert. She had already spoken to three other men before choosing him because she liked the answers he gave to her questions. They later met face to face, courted, and married. That was several years ago.

My friend admitted that they have had some serious challenges in their marriage, but they have also been seeing a marriage counsellor and trying to work things out. They are very optimistic and determined to make it work. Their problems are not because of how they met; they are the same ones all marriages encounter.

Just as I do not think that there is a single, designated partner for any individual, so also do I not think that there is a perfect partner for anyone. Marriage is all about two people willing to respect and love each other and work hard for their marriage. My husband and I are committed to our relationship and continue to work on it no matter what. In the end, the joy is in reaping what we sow. If we sow love, we reap love. If we sow hatred, we reap hatred. When people sow wisely, they reap the fruit of their labour. When they sow, they must wait patiently for things to grow. They should never look back in regret and wish that they had married another partner. They made a choice and their responsibility now is to work towards the success of their marriage.

While I cherish my husband and would not exchange him for another man, I believe that I would still have ended up with a fulfilling marriage, even if I had met and married a different man with the same basic qualities, beliefs, values, and commitment to the relationship as he has. I say this because success in marriage is based on the couple's level of commitment, patience, and sacrifice, which is what counts in any relationship.

The Different Stages of Marriage

As life goes through various seasons, so does marriage. Generally, couples go through predictable stages in marriage, although the intensity may vary, depending on individual personalities. For many, everything seems great, until the honeymoon is over. The marriage then takes on new meaning and unshakeable commitment becomes key to the success and stability of the relationship. I often meet ladies who feel that they made a mistake by marrying their current partner. They believe that their marriage would be better off today, if they had married so-and-so instead. This is often because the spark in their relationship has died. What they do not realise is that all marriages go through different stages, as attested by most psychologists and marriage experts. I have also experienced them in my own marriage. I am particularly drawn to the basic stages adapted from the works of Harville Hendrix, an experienced marriage and relationship expert.

Romantic Love

The romantic stage is so good that we wish it would last forever. Our hearts are filled with love and passion. This phase may last for the first two years. It is sometimes referred to as the stage of "loving under the influence". According to Hendrix, not only is the heart full of love, but the brain is also flooded with feel-good neurochemicals such as dopamine and phenylethylamine. Their effect on behaviour is the same as that of endorphin. Endorphin increases energy, feelings of well-being, a positive outlook, and sexual desire as well.

During this period, the relationship is characterised by deep romance. In many ways, it tallies with our fantasies about marriage. The desire to be together and share everything is strong, and so is the sexual attraction. It is common for someone to believe that their partner makes them shine, bringing out the best in them. This is a stage that does not last long enough. If that is your level now, enjoy it, but remember it is only for a season! I still remember going through this stage when I was electrified every time I was around my husband. He simply swept me off my feet.

In time, the feeling wears off, though. Sexual energies lessen to give way to energies for other responsibilities. When this happens, many couples wrongly assume that something has gone wrong and their relationship no longer works. They think that they are no longer in love with their partner because they do not feel the fire anymore. A wife may no longer feel attracted to her husband.

Disappointment, Distress, or Power Struggle

At this stage, disappointment, loneliness, regret, and other similar feelings associated with settling down are common. According to Hendrix, the decline of neurochemicals becomes evident and results in low sexual energies, too. Sex may become routine and not as enjoyable as it once was. Children—already born or expected—and increased responsibilities can give rise to all manner of reactions. Because of the challenges presented by this unavoidable stage, it is common for partners to reach out to past lovers at this point, opening the door to infidelity. However, finding a new partner is not the solution. Difficulties encountered must be used as learning experiences; they can unlock opportunities to deeper connections, intimacies, and fulfilment in the relationship.

Some couples can find this stage extremely challenging. Many of them feel they have worked so hard on the relationship and are not willing to give it much more attention; they are generally ready for a break! At this point, desperation, disappointment, and hopelessness set in. Many of the couples that I have interacted with at this stage claim that they have chosen to stay together simply because of the children.

At a relationship seminar that covered topics on relationships and fidelity, many participants were shocked to discover just how attached they still are to their past lovers. Some admitted receiving phone calls from them on a regular basis and exchanging emails and text messages. They loved to hear that their former lovers still thought about them. They were thrilled to experience once again that fantasy feeling, which sent tingles up and down their spines! Exciting, yes, but very dangerous to the marriage relationship.

Knowledge and Awareness

During this stage, people gain new information and insights about themselves and their partner. Things that were tolerable in the beginning become intolerable. The key to surviving this stage is to anticipate it and respond positively to its challenges. It is common for couples to stay together simply because they have children together or because of financial concerns, which makes them feel trapped. It is important to recognise that commitment to the marriage comes first and is reason enough to make it work.

At this point, both parties may be anxious, unhappy, and confused. They become aware that something is wrong and that they are in trouble if they do not work on the relationship and make changes. They also recognise that they have the power to choose whether to make the relationship work or not. They desire to rekindle their love and commitment to the marriage. They know that they alone can make the difference.

In this phase it is important for couples to search themselves, recognise their behaviour, and look at causes of conflicts to avoid them. It may also be necessary to involve a mentoring couple, if they had not already done so at the beginning of their marital journey. They should be honest with themselves and evaluate the marriage truthfully. It is important to cultivate the atmosphere of oneness. If the marriage is challenged, they should find materials on the subject and read widely; otherwise, and if necessary, they should consult a marriage counsellor.

Transformation

As couples begin to enjoy the benefits of a marriage that satisfies their needs, they enter the final stage. This stage is characterised by a more profound and lasting intimacy, resulting from years of sharing ups and downs. It is a period, which lives out the vision of the partnership and exercises unconditional love and the bond of "best friends". It is a time when couples work to keep it that way. At this time, the mature marriage should be consistent in deep love, success, and transformation.

Marriage is all about two people that are willing to learn to love each other and work out the conflicts and problems.

During this stage, spouses begin to accept each other for who they are and to accommodate one another's strengths and weaknesses. They choose to work together to renew their relationship, learning about their individual needs and managing their differences and areas of conflict. They learn to communicate effectively, creating emotional safety that becomes part of their healing. Consequently, the relationship grows. Somehow, it is much easier for them to work through challenges that come their way because they have made adjustments and developed mutual understanding and trust. They finally have realistic expectations of each other, accept the uniqueness of their partner, and cherish one another.

God has given us the opportunity to meet many people and experience a variety of relationships. We now have to choose the one relationship that works for us, the one that can lead to a fulfilling marriage. We can marry many suitable persons. Being fixated on one person, especially one who has neither respect nor interest in us, is not what God intends for us, though. He also has no desire to dictate upon us whom we should marry; He does not want us to blame Him afterwards when things fail to work out, just like Adam did. When He asked Adam why he ate fruit from the forbidden tree, Adam indirectly blamed God, when he blamed his God-given mate.

How to Select a Suitable Partner

Several years, ago, I had the privilege of attending the wedding of a close family friend's son in India. As is the custom among Hindus, the family had taken it upon themselves to find a bride for their firstborn son, Kirit. He had never met the girl; he had only seen pictures of her and had spoken to her over the phone. Although Kirit was educated and exposed to other cultures, he did not resist the family's initiative. He knew that when the time came, his parents would get him a suitable bride.

When the couple finally met, they went through various marriage rituals. It was one of the most beautiful ceremonies I had ever attended. It was exciting to witness the joining of these two young people who had never met before. That was over 10 years ago and they still enjoy a great marriage. They have learnt to love each other and to live together as a perfect match.

How did Kirit's parents determine the best bride for their son? The answer to this question provides us with the basic principles of finding a suitable partner. The family background was crucial; she had to be from a "good family". She had to share the same faith, values, and beliefs as Kirit's family had. She had to have achieved a particular level of education. Other social and economic qualities were also looked into, which would allow her and her husband to bond and flow together easily.

We see the same picture in the Old Testament story of Abraham and his beloved son Isaac. In those days, it was customary for a father to find a wife for his son. As Abraham wanted the best for Isaac, he did everything in his power to get him the perfect bride. Being too old to do it himself, he requested the chief servant of his household to go to Abraham's ancestral home and find Isaac a wife. The chief servant undertook the journey and did succeed in his quest. Isaac loved his wife Rebekah all his life.

I had the privilege of growing up with my paternal grandmother after whom I am named. She loved to talk and tell many stories. One day, I asked her how she met and married my grandfather. She told me that she had never met or dated grandpa before they began to live together. Her family and his knew one another, though. My grandfather's aunties abducted her and brought her home to be his wife. She never went back to her family. She settled down and bore him six children. She lived a full life and died at the ripe old age of 120 years.

In our many talks, my grandma shared with me the qualities her people, the Kikuyu, usually looked for in a bride or a groom. A family with a history of mental illness or one that produced thieves was out of the question. On the other hand, outstanding integrity and a respectable standing in the community were greatly valued. I give these examples to illustrate one point: The marriages of Kirit and his wife, Isaac and Rebekah, and my grandparents worked because the couples came together based on shared and respected family values. They accepted each other and worked together to allow their marriages to function, not only for their individual good but also for that of the family and the community. They understood that marriage is one of the most significant experiences of human life; it should not be entered into lightly. They realised that it is more about choosing to love and live with another person rather than just enjoying tingly feelings. They had learnt that sexual excitement alone cannot form the basis of selecting a life partner.

In summary, here are some things to bear in mind when looking for a suitable partner:

1. There is no one particular designated partner for any one individual.

2. People must have realistic expectations. Beyond mental fantasies, Prince Charming may not exist.

3. The spouse-to-be must have a family background of outstanding integrity and respect.

4. The potential husbands must share the same faith as their would-be wives.

5. Couples need to share similar and compatible visions and values.

6. They should be intellectually compatible with each other.

7. They must be socially and economically compatible.

8. Potential life partners must show readiness for commitment and hard work; their commitment should be evident in other areas of their lives.

9. None of the partners should enter the marriage bond due to desperation or other external pressures: the marriage decision should be made freely and willingly.

10. Marriage is part of God's plan for humanity. Therefore, you should involve God through prayer in all your marriage plans.

The following are signs of an unhealthy relationship:

1. Insecurity

2. Irrevocably broken trust

3. Feelings of hurt more than of joy

4. Lack of mutual respect

5. Frequent complaints about the relationship to others

6. Repeated lack of resolution of differences

7. Emotional or physical abuse

8. Lack of accommodation of partner's family and/or friends

9. Partner's desire for a baby before marriage

10. Dishonesty

Chapter Two

Successful Courtship

...I found the one my heart loves.
Song of Solomon 3:4

Courtship is the traditional dating period before engagement and marriage. During courtship, a couple get to know each other before deciding whether to take their relationship to the next level of commitment. Courtship is serious business, as it is the time for both parties to discern if the friendship can grow into a permanent relationship or not. Any possibility of marriage should be discussed and agreed upon and not merely assumed or implied.

Behaviour during Courtship

Today's courtship is referred to in terms such as "going out" and "seeing someone", among others. In my days, it used to be "going steady". Whatever you call it, courtship should be taken seriously because a lasting relationship may be formed at this time—a relationship based on reality, not fantasy. A real relationship is one where you love another person enough to be honest with him about who you are, what you plan to do, and about everything else. Some people fear that they may get married only to discover that they have no sexual or romantic feelings for each other. The temptation, therefore, is to "find out", before they commit. My conviction is that you should not be sexually involved with each other, or anyone else for that matter, until after marriage. This is the only way of ensuring that you only get involved with one partner in your lifetime. If you engage in sexual relations before the marital commitment, then there is the possibility of having several sexual partners, with all the pain and emotional baggage that it leaves behind.

> *A real relationship is one where you love another person enough to be honest with him about who you are,...and about everything else.*

If after the courtship and commitment to marriage no attraction or romance develops, I would be quite concerned. It is good to be attracted to someone, but it is not necessary; the feelings can grow. With time, it can become deeper than passion is, which wears off sooner than you know it. In my opinion, sexual attraction should follow as a natural consequence of the initial attraction and the growing feelings of romance and love. I can assure you that deep romantic love increases over time, as many older couples can also testify. Getting married on the love you feel in your 20s is not necessarily a good standard. Expect much more.

What to Consider in Courtship

Friendship, Friendship, Friendship!

A romantic relationship is a more intimate form of friendship. He must be a friend! If you are not friends, then you have to spend a lot of time and energy to develop a simple friendship, which can be complicated because of the many emotions involved. In courtship, you enter the first phase of marriage, so you need to know a few things about him and his character to make a rather important decision.

Communication is crucial to any friendship and, certainly, in marriage. It is important that you can communicate freely, transparently, and without fear of victimisation. Open communication is necessary in order to understand your partner fully. A popular song goes, "You can be a lover but not a friend". This should not happen to you. Above everything else, ensure that you are good friends.

Every time someone asks me how my husband and I have managed to stay married and happy for so many years, my response is usually simple: God has blessed us. Bob and I have been the best of friends since the start of our relationship. The strongest and most successful long-term relationships are those based on friendship. Ultimately, our purpose in being a friend should be to encourage, lift up, and help build the character of our friends. We should do all we can to assist them in achieving their dreams. Friendship does not begin after marriage; it begins at the courtship stage. It will become the foundation of the relationship.

Committed Christian

I emphasise "committed" because it is important. He must have the same values as yours. He should love God, enjoy going to church, take pleasure in serving others, and be a faithful and diligent member of his church and community. Accountability groups are very essential for a successful Christian life. If your partner does not embrace them, it will put extra strain on your relationship. It is also necessary to evaluate your value systems. Things that are vital to you may not be so to your partner.

Parental Involvement

Parents should assume their God-given responsibility to assist their children make wise marriage choices. This may sometimes include suggesting suitable candidates for marriage. It may include turning away some suitors and ruling out others. It is important for parents to understand courtship and play a part in supporting and mentoring their children during this crucial stage of their lives. Romantic love has been exalted beyond proportion. "Love" is often the sole reason given for marriage. With courtship, perhaps the overriding principle is wisdom, a virtue that parents possess in superior measure, especially when it comes to guiding their children. The role of parents therefore is to assist their children understand courtship. It is helpful at this stage to understand the power of attraction, the effects of infatuation, and the challenges of indulging in sex before marriage and the risks thereof. At this stage, it is important for parents to provide clear biblical guidelines before the couple's relationship begins.

I met a beautiful girl named Wanjiku in a marriage fitness seminar. She shared with me that her parents were very harsh and strict with her; they never allowed her to do anything she desired, whether pertaining to career, personal development, or a social life. The parents feared that she would fall into bad company, get pregnant, and bring shame upon the family. Wanjiku loved school and wanted to make a good life for herself, so she hung on, although she always felt restricted and oppressed.

At the age of 21, she decided to break free from the repressive atmosphere by finding a husband for herself. She met and married a respectable and successful man 12 years her senior. He was a father figure to her, who compensated for what she desired, but never received, from her own father.

Today she admits that she entered into the relationship with a sense of inadequacy and incompleteness, and much immaturity. She thinks that she probably should have taken more time to know her husband—and herself—better. "I did not know him well enough," she laments. "I should have given it more time. I thought he was the right partner. Now, I think otherwise. We do not agree on anything. He does not go to church with me, visit my parents, or associate with our friends. He is not involved in the home, will not help with the household chores, and does not take the children out or even to school."

Courting Duration

How long should a couple court before marriage? Should they wait for one, three, or five years? Should they marry instinctively?

Marriage is a lifelong commitment, so you should be ready before plunging in. Time alone cannot produce the necessary readiness. What matters most is evidence of maturity to tackle relationship challenges. Different relationships will need different time spans, depending on issues and challenges on hand.

During courtship, take note of unbecoming habits, attitudes, and behaviour towards each other because they will be carried into the marriage. The answers to the following general questions can be used to gauge the readiness of both parties to tie the knot:

- Can you entrust your innermost thoughts, dreams, and fantasies to each other?
- Have you known each other long enough to have reasonable knowledge of your partner?
- What are his personal experiences?
- What are his family and personal backgrounds? Will they affect compatibility?
- Do you share the same vision and goals?
- What is your motive for settling down?
- Are you emotionally connected to each other?

Maina has been in a relationship with his girlfriend for the last seven years. As much as he feels the need to marry and settle down, he believes he cannot do so because his current job cannot guarantee a comfortable life for his family. He says he will wait until a better job comes along. In the meantime, his girlfriend Njoki feels she is running out of time. She will soon turn 34 and Maina still holds on to the engagement ring.

Both Maina and Njoki have no doubt that they want to spend the rest of their life together, but financial security is important to Maina. While this is commendable, no one can ever be fully ready for marriage. Some things will just have to grow alongside the marriage. Long courtships that last over five years can be risky; they may result in boredom and a broken relationship. It is common for them to fall eventually by the wayside.

Marriage is a lifelong commitment, so you should be ready before plunging in.

Early in our marriage, my husband gave me a birthday card that read, "You taught me to love you, but I would have gone ahead and done it on my own anyway!" Those words had a different meaning at that time. Later in life, though, their significance became a reality. We develop in relationships. In time, we learn to love deeply because we feel safe and can trust. We feel understood, cared for, and, most of all, respected, regardless of our shortcomings.

In conclusion, the length of the dating period does not determine readiness. What is important is the established strength and stability of the relationship. As long as it is based on friendship, love, respect and mutual understanding, and offers opportunity for growth, the couple can get married any time, as long as they seek the guidance, counsel and blessings from their parents, mentors, and spiritual leaders. The foundation of any good relationship is true friendship.

Falling in Love and Marriage

'Falling in love' is a strong instinctive attraction to a person of the opposite sex. It is based on feelings, which may not always be shared or reciprocated. However, when the feeling is mutual, then both parties get together and grow in love. Falling in love is hard to explain, at least to most people; it is not cognitive but usually physical and emotional. In her attempt to explain her feelings upon falling in love, one lady Jane had this to say:

> *We met at a friend's party. The minute our eyes locked, that was it! My whole body went numb; I knew I was crazy about the man and I wanted him for myself. That evening, we spent time together and it felt like we had always known each other. I wanted him in my arms and, against my better judgement, in my bed! How can I explain it? The feelings of ecstasy were overwhelming.*

Maria, on the other hand, does not remember falling in love, although she loves her husband deeply. For her, it was a friendship that eventually grew into a romantic love relationship.

People fall in love for many reasons. What is considered attractive varies considerably from one culture to another and from one individual to another. For Solomon, it was simple: "I found the one my heart loves." (Song of Solomon 3:4a) Many scholars from various disciplines have tried to understand romantic love, and much has been written on this subject, but it still remains a mystery.

I love to speak to, mentor, inspire, and encourage brides as they undertake the journey of marriage. Something awakens within me whenever I speak to a couple intent on marrying. They remind me of my own thrill and excitement many years ago, when I fell in love with my "Prince Charming". The feeling was incredible, indescribable, and electrifying – a "tilting-over" feeling. No wonder someone came up with the phrase "to fall head over heels in love!"

At a celebration that my husband and I attended with our friends, we were asked to explain what had attracted us to our spouses. We laughed and cried, as we shared around the table. Beautiful hair, a full bust, beauty, and charisma were some of the traits mentioned. It was actually my first time to hear from Bob that my "great pair of legs and figure" had attracted him to me. It was hilarious. As for me, he fitted into my fantasy of Prince Charming: tall, dark, and handsome!

Feelings and physical attraction have their place in marriage, but they do not always count. Looks do not make the man. My mother used to say to me in my mother tongue, "Uthaka nduriaguo", which translates to "Good looks are not eaten". I thought she was being cruel and mean when she said that to me, but today I echo her words often. External looks should not be the basis of a relationship. Yes, there ought to be some mutual attraction and physical appearance does play a role in it. It is, however, not comparable to inward beauty. It must not be allowed to take priority over the spiritual and mental aspects of your relationship. Never lose a promising relationship just because someone is not as tall, dark, or handsome as you would like him to be.

A while ago, I attended a very interesting wedding ceremony. Both bride and groom were not physically present. They were doing it in England, while those of us in Kenya witnessed the proceedings on a large screen at the residence of the bride's parents. In the midst of all the activities, an aunt of the bride had a chance to speak with her over the live video feed, "Wanja, you have met many good-looking and charismatic gentlemen in your life. Now that you have finally chosen your life partner, could you tell us what made you settle for John?"

There was dead silence as everyone waited for her answer. Wanja rolled her eyes and played nervously with her fingers. Suddenly, she looked up and said, "Auntie, I cannot tell you why I chose to marry John. All I know is that something like electricity did it for me!"

Everyone burst out laughing. I could not help but wonder what my own response would have been had I been asked the same question. When I met Bob, we connected instantly; I had the same experience of "electricity" as Wanja had. He and I were not introduced to each other by anyone. Our eyes had locked together at a wedding ceremony, where he was taking photographs. That was it. It was instant attraction that developed into a passionate courtship, which culminated in marriage three years later.

When we said "I do", all I knew then was that I was about to spend the rest of my life with a man I was crazy about, who would share my life in the most intimate way, and who would be there for me always. The thought excited me and I had good reason to look forward to all that. My parents were very strict. I was not allowed to spend much time with my lover during our courtship, so I looked forward to sleeping with him, waking up with him, playing with him, and doing things with him all the time. The climax of it all for me was having children with him.

Electricity aside, I knew that marriage was a journey into the unknown. At that time, all I knew about it was what I had observed from my parents' marriage and those of other couples close to them. Sadly, what I had seen so far was not good. If that was all there was to marriage, I would have chosen to remain single the rest of my life. Theirs was a very stormy relationship; it certainly did not fit into my idea of a good marriage. I wanted mine to be different. I wanted to love and be loved, to make a good home and have great kids whom I would treat better than I had been treated.

I did not grow up in an environment where love was expressed. It was considered a sign of weakness. Others considered it an influence of the West, which could not be tolerated. I craved to be held, to be hugged, to touch and be touched. The first opportunity to experience this kind of love seemed too precious to let go. I wanted it to last a lifetime. King Solomon—described as the wisest man who ever lived—knew the value of love and said, "Enjoy life with your wife, whom you love..." (Ecclesiastes 9:9)

Looking back today, though, I think my parents were going through a challenging stage of their marriage at that time. At the age I was in, I expected marriage to be romantic all throughout, so I assumed they were not happily married.

Some Quick Tips

As you seek Mr Right, never become desperate or appear to be. There are many potential partners around. Your duty is to know and focus on the values you expect in a partner. As long as you have the same values and beliefs, share the same faith, and have the same life aspirations, you will most likely make it together.

The key to finding the right partner is to identify qualities that you can hold on to as nonnegotiable standards and then evaluate the potential suitors against them. As marriage involves two people, the assessment cannot be one-sided. The other person will also have expectations. What are your ideals and goals in life? You need to determine them and then find out what the other person wants. Are your goals and objectives in harmony with each other's expectations?

Pray and seek the Lord's guidance in this direction. God is faithful and will grant you the desires of your heart. He will not pick a specific partner for you, though. You have to do that yourself. God will guide you along the way. Pray for the spirit of discernment, so that you may be alert. Pay attention to details. If you do not feel a connection with someone, leave him alone. There needs to be chemistry between the two of you. And be patient. Finding a marriage partner is not an emergency. Do not be pressured by what is happening in the lives of your peers. Rushing into a relationship because of peer pressure, parental coercion, or otherwise is the last thing you should do. Take your time. If you make a wrong move, you will live to regret it the rest of your life. Marriage requires total commitment and faithfulness to the one you choose.

Marriage does not miraculously cure weaknesses of character. The "minor" things that you let your partner get away with during courtship can end up becoming the monsters that destroy your marriage.

The following are definite warning signs which should not be ignored:
- Physical abuse (no matter how slight)
- Emotional abuse
- Disrespect
- Financial mismanagement or unaccountability

- Alcohol abuse
- Drug abuse
- Irresponsibility
- Excessive and insensitive socialising
- Infidelity, and
- Untrustworthiness

Mary dated her husband for 10 years, three of which they spent living together. After one year of marriage, however, she left him. When I asked her the reason, she told me that he was unfaithful. He would leave the house supposedly to "buy a newspaper", "have his car washed", or "see a friend" and end up spending the night out. Sometimes, he would disappear for an entire weekend. Her friends would report seeing him in a nightclub, with a girl. In the end, she could not take it anymore. It turned out that this man had always been unfaithful, but Mary believed he would change once they got married.

Beloved, hear me and hear me well: If your relationship does not work out at the courtship level, forget it. It will never work at the level of marriage. If he does not go to church with you during courtship, he will not do so in marriage. If he is irresponsible now, he will remain so. If he cheats today, he will continue tomorrow.

Do not settle for anything just to be married. I often hear many women say, "My biological clock is ticking and I need to have someone, before it is too late. We have been dating for some time now, so I had better stick with him. I do not think I can find someone else." Why consign yourself to lifelong misery? Let that clock tick a little longer instead of spending your life with a man whose name spells "trouble". Believe in yourself and trust God to grant your heart's desires. Make yourself look attractive and available for dating. Someone else may be looking at you and desiring a relationship but is put off by your present entanglement.

Testing Your Love

Was yours love at first sight or infatuation? Many have said that they fell in love on the first date or have always loved someone for many years even before that someone approached them. I would now like to explore the subject of love.

What is love? 1 Corinthians 13:4-7 says that love is not a feeling; it should be based on actions:

Love is patient, love is kind. It does not envy, it does not boast, it is not proud. It does not dishonour others, it is not self-seeking, it is not easily angered, it keeps no record of wrongs. Love does not delight in evil but rejoices with the truth. It always protects, always trusts, always hopes, always perseveres.

If love is not a feeling, then what is it about love that blows our minds? What is it about love that drives us nuts?

Many times, wives have accused their men of not being romantic. The African man is accused particularly of not displaying affection in the manner that their wives expect. According to the men, though, love is not a display of warmth but an action that involves making their wife comfortable and providing for her material needs. I like what M. Scott Peck says about love in his book *The Road Less Travelled*: "One result of the mysterious nature of love is that no one has ever arrived at a satisfactory definition of love" (1978, 69). In his view, "love is too large, too deep ever to be truly understood or measured or limited within the framework of words".

Since the English word "love" is used so broadly, it is helpful to distinguish between its different types to have a more precise understanding of the New Testament's message. The New Testament was written in Greek, so it does include the various Greek words for love. The Greeks were passionate about their expression of love and categorised it in different ways, depending on its usage. Their language has four distinct words for it: *philia, eros, storge,* and *agape.*

Philia

We recognise *philia* and its meaning from the name Philadelphia: the city of brotherly love. It includes friendships and the fellowship of people you enjoy being with. Although *philia* is wonderful, it is not reliable, since it is held captive by the shifting sands of situations, as well as by changing perceptions and expectations. Unfortunately, we probably all know of a friendship that waned or was completely severed because of time, distance, harsh words, misinterpreted actions, etc. When the New Testament commends love, *philia* is not the word used.

Eros

Eros is passionate love, with sensual desire and longing. The modern Greek word, *erotas,* means "romantic love". It does not have to be sexual in nature. It is the passionate love, which drives the relationship in the beginning. It is great love and is healthy; it is essential in the expression of the marital relationship. This love is based mostly on feelings. It is what Wanja and others describe as "electricity". It is temporary and does not last forever. When you are at the stage of erotic love, it is easy to confuse the feeling with something else. There is a thin line between reality and fantasy.

Storge

Storge means "affirmation" in Greek. It is a natural affection, fondness through familiarity, especially felt by parents for offspring and, generally, among family members. This love happens without any coercion.

Agape

Agape refers to the paternal love of God for man and love of man for God. However, it is also extended to include brotherly love for all humanity. This is the highest level of love. It is the love demonstrated by Jesus Christ on the cross, when He died for our sins. It should replace *eros* in a marriage relationship that grows towards oneness. *Agape* love is not based on the physical but on the spiritual and emotional. It is selfless; it is continually shown through action as described in 1 Corinthians 13. All marriages should strive towards this love.

Finding the one whom your soul loves is good but keeping the love you find is precious. Keep the flame burning!

Chapter Three

This Is Not the Man I Married!

Love is something eternal; the aspect may
change but not the essence.
Vincent van Gogh

Thirty-plus years have passed, but my memories are still fresh: The day came when I was finally ready to marry the love of my life. There would be no more missing him, no more waiting for his letters, and no more longing for dates that seemed years apart. I would have Bob all to myself, all the time. It did not matter that I would no longer wake up in the same house as my parents or siblings. All that mattered was the life I was about to begin with the one I loved.

At that time, I would not have believed anyone who would have told me that my love and I would disagree on or fight about anything. I knew husbands and wives disagreed, fought, and even divorced. I believed that happened because they did not love each other enough or never even loved each other in the first place. Bob and I loved each other dearly. That would never happen to us.

The Fights Begin

I clearly remember our first fights, just as clearly as I do our wedding day.

Coming home late was not a big deal for Bob. I found that unacceptable. What was even more challenging was that when he came late, he always expected me to wake up, leaving my already warm bed, to heat up his food, serve him, and keep him company while he ate. Oh, how I minded! One day, he came home late again. This time, I decided not to wake up and serve him dinner. After all, he could do it himself. When he tried to get me up to serve him, I was ready for him. "Go get it yourself!" I protested. "Why didn't you eat wherever you were? It's past supper time!"

When I was growing up, I never once saw my mother serve food to my father after bedtime. The unwritten house rule was that no supper was to be served after a certain time. Everyone always assumed that latecomers had already eaten wherever they had been. Dad knew this, so he never bothered Mum. Instead, he always woke me up to warm his food or to cook the meat he brought with him. At times, he would bring home a whole gazelle, accidentally knocked down on his way home. We then had to slaughter the animal the same night to preserve the meat. There were many occasions, when I had to go to the kitchen garden late at night to get coriander and green pepper to spice the meat. I loved my sleep, but I loved Dad more, so I did it with pleasure. In my own marriage, however, I did not intend to wake up in the dead of the night. I thought Bob would have to wait until his daughter was old enough to warm his food.

On his part, Bob had come from a completely different background. His mother would not go to bed before serving dinner to her husband, regardless of his time of arrival. He expected the same in our marriage. His experiences and expectations inevitably clashed with mine, leading to disagreements and arguments that finally exploded into a nasty conflict.

Birthdays were always special occasions for me growing up; I celebrated every birthday. It was a time when I received the greatest affirmation from my parents, siblings, extended family, and friends. My 10th birthday was particularly memorable because my mother made me a two-tier cake. She invited many guests and I received many gifts. Even after I left home, my father always sent me a birthday card, a gift, and some money to celebrate it. I treasure those cards and keep all of them to this day. I grew up knowing that remembering someone's birthday was actually saying to the person, "I'm so glad you were born. It's a privilege not only to know you but also to have a relationship with you."

Bob did not care about birthdays or any other special occasion. They were never celebrated in his home, so he attached no value to them. On several instances, I explained to him how much I valued birthdays, but he still forgot my birthday several times. Important dates like anniversaries, Christmas, and New Year were also very significant to me and my family. Again, these meant little to him; I spent our first Christmas and New Year without him. Thank God that this quickly passed. Constant reminders, diary entries, and an expression of my needs finally helped make momentous dates a part of our family tradition.

Of course, you can imagine the hell I raised! I did not talk to him for days. I was ready to return to my mother's house and forget the marriage, but she was unwilling to have me back. According to her, two married women cannot share the same house. She reminded me that I had married the man of my dreams, so I had to sort out the issues with him. I thought I would die; I thought my world had crumbled. I thought my lover had become my worst enemy. In time, however, I realised this was not so.

This lack of preparation for marital conflict was not peculiar to me. Most couples enter into marriage, believing that they will never fight over anything because they love each other. The truth is that any two people placed together for whatever reason will, at one time or another, experience conflict just because they are different from each other. They come into the relationship with diverse expectations. Look at politicians, for example; they always clash with each other. Even siblings with the same parents experience the same thing. Pastors on the same staff also have disagreements. If people in these situations go through conflict, how much more would two people whose lives are literally intertwined!

As a young wife, I would sometimes share my marital woes with my mother. She would respond to my complaints with a Kikuyu proverb that says, *"Mathanwa me kîondo kîmwe matiagaga gûkong'orana"*. (Two axes in the same basket will inevitably knock against one another.) A married couple is definitely "two axes in the same basket", so the husband and wife will certainly knock against each other.

Marital conflict is not necessarily a bad thing. It can help one partner get to know the other better. It can help them know one another's likes and dislikes and be conscious of behaviours to avoid in the future. Handled properly, it can promote growth and greater closeness in a relationship. If conflict is mismanaged, however, it can destroy the relationship, regardless of the couple's intimacy. Even when conflict is caused by sin and leads to a great deal of stress, God can still use it for the good (Romans 8:28).

In time, the initial excitement of marriage gives way to responsibilities. With children, mortgage repayments, and other duties to take care of, stress is bound to build up. It can eat away the energy for romance in the relationship. As frustrations increase, misunderstandings will occur, leading to tension and conflicts.

Know Your Partner

One of the greatest books I have read and that revolutionised my thoughts about relationships is *The Five Love Languages* by Gary Chapman. I learnt from the book that people appreciate love through different "emotional languages". An emotional language is behaviour or actions that communicate a sense of being loved to an individual. Various people understand love in different ways: through acts of service, quality time, gifts, touch, or affirmation.

I was able to identify my own and my husband's languages of love. For me, words of affirmation and gifts are the languages by which love is communicated to me. When I am affirmed, I feel loved and valued. And the thought that someone went out of his way, shopped around, and zeroed in on a particular gift for me makes me happy. The personalised gift tells me that he took time to think about me. That speaks volumes and is indeed my other language of love.

My husband feels loved when I take time to do things for him. He loves it when I go out of my way to make him a good meal because he enjoys good food. He appreciates a clean, tidy, and well-kept home. He notices any redecoration, no matter how slight. He always notices when I make the bed, clean up the drawers, and tidy up his clothes because he loves an orderly house. He also appreciates some attention and tender loving care.

I do all these for my husband because I know what he wants. He has either expressed it or clearly indicated to me what he appreciates. Spouses need to express their individual expectations with one another as a way of avoiding most disagreements and disputes. Expression should be followed by a mutual commitment to see promises through. A couple's failure to identify their partner's love language is the source of many marital conflicts, so take time to discover what works for your partner.

When I was young, my friends and I would often make "cross my heart and hope to die" promises to one another. We were committed to keeping our promises because breaking them meant death! I felt secure in the mutual agreement that we respected. From those childhood commitments, I learnt that making and keeping agreements is important. Every marriage needs that sense of safety, security, and togetherness from the knowledge that promises will be kept.

Unfortunately, in many marriages, agreements are often implied rather than expressed clearly. People often assume that their partner will figure out what they need and respond accordingly. When their expectations are unmet, it results in disappointment and mistrust. State your expectations clearly, not only to your spouse but also to your entire household.

They need to know what you expect of them, so they can tell if they live up to your expectations. Whenever someone complains that their loved one never does things for them, I usually ask them whether they have ever expressed that need clearly to their partner. More often than not, they have not. You cannot measure performance if there are no criteria or stated expectations. When your expectations are not met, do not lose heart, keep working at it, and you will eventually win.

Spouses need to express their individual expectations with one another as a way of avoiding most disagreements and disputes.

The differences between women and men are not only well-documented but are also often talked about. There are actual differences in the way women's and men's brains are structured and in their reactions to events and stimuli. Popular marriage counsellor and seminar leader John Gray, in his book *Men Are From Mars, Women are From Venus*, articulates this very well. He provides practical and proven ways for men and women to communicate and relate better by acknowledging the differences between them. God intended it to be this way: He created them male and female.

When women encounter a problem, their tendency is to talk about what happened, while men are interested in what needs to be done. Early in my marriage, I noticed that whenever I came to my husband with a situation, he showed little interest in the details. I was interested in them, however, because I wanted him to hear my heart, so he could show he cared for me and was concerned. I finally realised that he was not interested in them; he was interested in providing a solution. In the middle of my heartrending account, he would interrupt and ask, "So what would you like me to do, Jennie?"

Sometimes I wish he would join me in my pity party and mourn with me, hear me, and feel my pain. In time, though, I came to understand that he would rather set me free from the pain rather than help me bask in it. Since his desire is to end my anguish, I have learnt to come to him with a specific action plan. Men may not listen to our details of pain, but they love us enough to see us out of the pain as soon as possible. For this reason, they want to solve the issues quickly while avoiding any further emotional entanglements.

For a long time in our marriage, I assumed that my husband would read my thoughts. Instead of making my needs known, I would hint at them, hoping he would figure them out and meet them. He usually never did, which led to much disappointment and distress. In time, I have become wiser. I have learnt to express my needs clearly, so they are met as I desired them to be met. I used to worry about asking him to drop off the children at school or to take one of them to hospital, when I could not take time off from work. When I finally asked, however, he was glad to help.

It was not an easy lesson to learn, but the breakthrough came when I accused him of not helping with responsibilities at home. His response shocked me. In his words, it had never occurred to him that I needed help because I was so good at doing everything. Besides, I had never asked for help, so he assumed I did not need any. From then on, I learnt to ask for assistance. The man in your life may look at you as a superwoman, so you need to let him know when you require a hand. He will be glad to assist.

Exercise

Here is a simple exercise that can be a big eye-opener in your mutual relationship. Below is a list of words that represent varying emotional needs and expectations. Go through them and circle the words that represent something important to you in your relationship. You can rate their importance from five to 10, with 10 being the most important. Feel free to add words that represent something that has not been included. If possible, have your partner go through the same exercise as well. Armed with each other's response, sit down and discuss them. You will be amazed at the number of scales that will fall off your eyes, regarding your partner and, perhaps, even yourself.

Acceptance	Gentleness	Responsibility
Admiration	Gratitude	Security
Appreciation	Honesty	Sensitivity
Balance	Individuality	Sensuality
Caring	Integrity	Sex
Commitment	Liveliness	Shared Experiences
Common interests	Love	Shared Values
Communication	Maturity	Sincerity
Compatibility	Non-possessiveness	Stability
Compromise	Openness	Supportiveness
Fairness	Passion	Tact
Family	Patience	Tolerance
Flexibility	Playfulness	Trust
Forgiveness	Politeness	Virtue
Friendship	Practicality	Warmth
Fun	Reassurance	Others
Generosity	Respect	

There Is No Turning Back

In my marriage, I have never spent a night away from my matrimonial home to let off steam and get over a conflict. I must admit that my mother played a major role in this. She made it clear to me that marriage was not just something I could try and discard at will. I had made my decision and I had to stick to it. She was not about to welcome me back home. I was still very young when I decided to get married rather than pursue a career. My family was disappointed at my decision, so I had to face the challenges ahead. I had to make the marriage work.

I cried many times. One of my rituals for letting off steam was to soak in the bathtub and weep all I wanted. My bath salts were my own tears. It helped me release tension without involving anyone. I made my decisions there. One thing was not debatable: I would make my marriage work. I was totally committed to it, which resulted in my husband and me developing a healthy way of dealing with and resolving conflicts.

Just as wine gets better with age, so did my relationship—and so should yours. Bob and I learnt to be honest with one another, to communicate our hurts to each other, and to discuss them. When I would be deeply offended by something that my husband was unaware of, I mentioned it. I realised that what appeared big to me appeared insignificant to him. Only by talking about my feelings did I receive his help in melting away the pain.

It is important to let your partner know when something bothers you. Many women tend to keep quiet and sulk, assuming that their partner ought to know what the problem is. Often, the offending partner has no clue about his wrongdoing, so he will label you as overreacting. Talk things out; do not let things build up. Unexpressed hurt eventually explodes, causing great damage. How do you expect to solve a problem if it has not been expressed? Scripture warns us not to let the sun go down without resolving issues (Ephesians 4:26).

When sharing hurts and disappointments, we need to be careful about how and when we do this. Sometime back, there was a piece of advice shared to the bride in almost every wedding ceremony I attended: "When your husband comes home and you are upset, fill your mouth with a glassful of water. Let it remain in your mouth, until you are ready to go to bed. That way, you will not speak a word to him no matter how provoked you are."

The advice is overdramatic, but the point is clear. It is wise not to speak when you are angry. While it is a good idea, it does not mean that you should sweep issues under the carpet. You must resolve anything that bothers you; do not allow accumulation. A helpful scriptural handle that can spare you much pain and unhappiness is "In your anger, do not sin. Do not let the sun go down while you are still angry, and do not give the devil a foothold." (Ephesians 4:26-27)

Not many conflicts can be solved by a five-minute chat, so it is wise to commit to working out your conflicts no matter how long it takes. This effort might save your marriage. Whatever the squabbles are all about, give your partner a chance to air his views without interruption, even if you do not agree with what he says. By listening carefully to him, you show that you value him; you are willing to consider his opinion. In responding to an angry reaction, remember that "A gentle answer turns away wrath, but a harsh word stirs up anger" (Proverbs 15:1). Reply to anger with a gentle voice, a relaxed posture, and calm gestures. Communicate in every way that you take the other's expression of anger seriously and want to resolve the problems that prompt it. Plan responses to possible objections; deal with them specifically and reasonably.

Not every offence needs discussion and resolution. Some couples tend to dwell on petty issues and injustices repeatedly. I used to be guilty of this because I had certain expectations, and when they were not met, my tendency was to become angry. I would find it difficult to let go of an offence, no matter how minor. I believed that nobody should get away with wrongdoing, a belief influenced by my upbringing. Through the years, the Lord has helped me develop patience; I am now better able to overlook offences. When we focus on what goes on in our own hearts rather than in our partner's, we are able to reason and deal better with our feelings. Our heart is the wellspring of all our thoughts, words, and actions, hence, the source of conflicts. "For out of the heart come evil thoughts—murder, adultery, sexual immorality, theft, false testimony, slander." (Matthew 15:19)

Many disputes are so insignificant that they can be resolved without addressing them. We can choose to overlook the offence deliberately and ask God to give us patience under the circumstances. "A person's wisdom yields patience; it is to one's glory to overlook an offence." (Proverbs 19:11) Overlooking an offence is a form of forgiveness; it involves a deliberate decision to let go of the wrongdoing, never to bring it up in the future while dealing with other transgressions. Dwelling on offences only makes us bitter and angry.

People handle conflict in different ways. Mwende believes in "nil by mouth", when she is upset. She will say nothing to her partner for a week and, in some cases, even a whole month. She cannot trust herself to say anything positive, when she is upset. To avoid an all-out conflict, she chooses to stay away and say nothing.

Njeri, on the other hand, goes into a destructive streak, when she gets upset. To hurt her husband, she destroys his suits. Her husband is very self-conscious and dresses immaculately. To get his attention, she chooses to hurt him where he is bound to feel it the most. She takes a pair of scissors and cuts his suits into quarters. By the time they decided to seek help, she had already destroyed more than 20 suits, leaving her husband with little to wear to the office!

Causes of Marital Conflicts

Conflict is a reality in all marriages. If you have not already been in conflict, then you can be sure that one will inevitably come your way. How you deal with conflict is the ultimate test of your commitment to the relationship. Conflicts cause people either to explode or to bury their feelings. Some are very responsive to anger and are quick react to their spouse, when a conflict surfaces. On the other hand, others avoid conflict at all costs. They bury their hurt deep in their hearts and carry around a volcano of bottled anger, until an opportune time comes, which may take days or even months to deal with.

Most marital conflicts can be traced to our individual temperaments, personality differences, and childhood experiences. We are who we are because of our family backgrounds, and the environment and company around which we grew up. As we mature, some of our experiences, particularly painful ones, tend to stick to us. Disappointment, fear, rejection, guilt, or even shame tends to hide deep in us while influencing our behaviour. These negative feelings are not pleasant and may cause us to project a false image. On the other hand, temperament plays a major role in our personalities. For this reason, it is helpful to understand some basics about temperaments.

Psychologists have identified four basic temperaments that can help us understand our personality and temperamental differences: choleric, melancholic, phlegmatic, and sanguine.

Four Basic Temperaments

Choleric

The choleric types make great leaders. They have much capacity for success, but they step on many toes to get there. They are extremely dynamic and active and have a compulsive need for change. They are strong-willed and decisive; they feel the need to correct every wrong. They are not easily discouraged. They exude confidence and can run anything. Socially, the choleric have little need for friends, but they work better in group activity. They lead and organise well. They excel, especially in emergencies.

However, all these come at a price. Because the cholerics thrive on opposition, they tend to be bossy, impatient, and quick-tempered. They find it difficult to relax. They enjoy controversies and arguments; they will not give up, even when they are clearly losing. They come on too strongly and can be quite unsympathetic. They tend to dominate others and have a know-it-all attitude. They may often be right but are unpopular.

Melancholic

The melancholic types are deep and thoughtful, with an unquenchable thirst for knowledge. They are prone to genius, with very creative minds. They are often talented, artistic, or musical. They can also be philosophical and poetic. They appreciate beauty and are self-sacrificing and sensitive to others. They often sacrifice their own will for others. They are perfectionists, often setting high standards. They want everything done right. If they were husbands, their homes would be in good order and their children well taken care of. They avoid drawing attention to themselves. They are faithful and devoted to whatever they do. They listen to complaints and can solve others' problems. They are cautious when making friends and are content to stay in the background. They are compassionate and are easily moved to tears. They tend to seek ideal mates.

The negative side of the melancholic is that they keep records of wrongs for a long time. They are moody and have a capacity for depression. They seem to enjoy being hurt because they have a persecution complex. They project false humility, are self-centred, have selective hearing, and are too introspective. Often, their expectations are beyond reach and may discourage their partners because they want everything done perfectly. They sulk over disagreements and make their partners feel guilty. They are socially insecure, withdrawn, and critical of others. They hold back affection and dislike those who oppose them. They are suspicious of others and are often unforgiving and full of contradictions. They do not accept compliments easily.

Phlegmatic

Phlegmatic types are low-keyed, calm, and unemotional. They are generally self-content and kind. They are easygoing, very consistent, relaxed, rational, curious, and observant. They often make good administrators and diplomats. They seek peace all the time, avoiding strife at all costs. Like the sanguine personality, they have many friends. However, they are more reliable, faithful, and compassionate than the sanguine are. They keep their emotions well hidden. They are patient and well-balanced. They do not easily get upset and can take both the good and the bad. They are easy to get along with. They are pleasant, inoffensive, and good listeners.

On the negative side, phlegmatic types are unenthusiastic and fearful at home. They avoid responsibility and are shy and selfish. They can be stubborn and set in their ways. They are lax on discipline and do not organise the home. They stay uninvolved and unexcitable; they generally like to have plenty of rest, which they never seem to have enough of. Their personality makes them lazy and resistant to change while inhibiting enthusiasm in others. The phlegmatic annoy the choleric, as they cannot be coerced into doing something they do not want.

Sanguine

The sanguine types have an appealing personality. They are talkative, fun-loving—usually the life of the party, and tend to attract others to themselves. They are full of ambition, energy, and passion, and they try to instil their passion in others. They have a great sense of humour. They are emotional and expressive, often cheerful and bubbling over. They also have a large capacity for curiosity. They are sincere at heart and are usually childlike. They can dominate people of other temperaments, especially phlegmatic types. On the social side, they make friends easily, love people, and thrive on compliments. They do not hold grudges and tend to apologise without hesitation. There is no dull moment with them and they flourish on spontaneous activities.

Awareness of your personality type helps you understand yourself and your reactions.

On the negative side, they leave in the middle of a chore or assignment, if they find something else more interesting or fun. They never want to grow up. They are compulsive talkers. They also tend to exaggerate and elaborate, dwelling on trivialities. They often have loud voices and laugh loudly. They allow themselves to be controlled by circumstances and are egotistical. They can be arrogant, cocky, and indulgent, thriving on fantasies. They hate being alone and need to occupy the centre stage. They love popularity and receiving credit. They make poor listeners and are often time wasters.

As you went through these personalities, you may have noticed that while individuals largely fit into one personality type, they also have bits of the other personalities. Awareness of your personality type helps you understand yourself and your reactions. Knowing your partner's personality type helps you understand why he does what he does, reacting in the manner he does. It will help you become more aware of the dynamics of strengths and weaknesses, where both of you are concerned. To some extent, it helps you become more patient and understanding. It may be useful to take a personality test to see where you fall.

Like most people, Joyce's opinion and viewpoint has always been important. Her principal temperament is choleric, a dose of melancholic, with a touch of sanguine. Given her nature of being a winner, it is important that she emerges the winner in any argument. However, she confesses her lesson that winning arguments has led to devastating losses elsewhere. She has learnt, therefore, that it is better to lose an argument and stay friends.

I could not agree more with Joyce. You may be right, but it is more important to respect others' viewpoint, even when you are persuaded of their wrong. Marriage-breaking differences occur because we never allow for the feelings and thoughts of our partners. No matter how eloquently you argue, you cannot force the other person to see things from your point of view.

Temperaments play a major role in behaviour. Interestingly, however, people suppress them during the courtship period. They do not allow small things to get in the way, nor do they allow annoying habits to become an issue. After the marriage, though, what one put up with before is no longer bearable. The personality they fell in love with becomes the person they now would rather hate. The passion of love quickly turns into a passion of hate.

It is often said that men are hunters; once they have their prey, they relax. After marriage, men generally do not go out of their way because they already have what they wanted. I could not deal with this. I had waited to be married with much anticipation, so I could do what I wanted to do and be where I wanted to be with my husband. Then suddenly, I could not find him, although during courtship, he always wanted my company and always had a plan. Now he was too busy with the boys to accommodate me, or so I thought.

Our love language changes as we transition from courtship to marriage and this sometimes sends the wrong signals. The attention, gifts, acts of service, words of affirmation, and touch we were once accustomed to may become different. The frequent dates and so on all but disappear. The reality of marriage is about acquiring new responsibilities, which brings along a change in lifestyle. Keep that in mind, as you try to figure out if he is still the man you married.

Life and marriage are not static; they evolve and you cannot always anticipate the various stages. What attracted you to the person changes with time and so does your value system. When you understand that you are unique and different from your partner, you begin to see clearly that he cannot behave like you or do things in the same manner. A gift of partnership is the capacity to bring the uniqueness of each individual into play to benefit the other.

Jane is not outgoing and does not make friends easily. Her husband George, however, makes and retains friendships. When Jane recognised her husband is sanguine and, therefore, the life of the party, she no longer felt insecure about him talking to everyone and taking centre stage. George, on the other hand, finally understood his wife's temperament. Initially, he had challenges in dealing with her overbearing and domineering manner, but his eyes were opened later.

Communicate, Communicate, Communicate!

Healthy communication is a vital ingredient of a successful marriage. Communicate with each other with gentleness, kindness, concern, love, and care. "Do not let any unwholesome talk come out of your mouths, but only what is helpful for building others up according to their needs, that it may benefit those who listen." (Ephesians 4:29)

If you keep things to yourself, then you destroy your relationship. "Make every effort to keep the unity of the Spirit through the bond of peace." (Ephesians 4:3) Develop the habit of sharing your thoughts, fears, feelings, and day's activities. Do not stop there; get interested in how your own man spent his day. This way you communicate that you care and are interested in the things that affect him. It also helps to develop an interest in your partner's hobbies or sports. You can then understand him, when he explains the victories and disappointments of his day.

For a long time, I never took any interest in my husband's sports. Bob has always loved them and spends a lot of time playing one of them. My lack of interest meant that I always felt left out. When I finally developed an interest in his pastime, I began to understand him whenever he went into a game's details: how it went, what he did, where he failed, and where he enjoyed himself. Eventually, I began to join him in his games, so we now have even more to talk about other than work and children.

If you develop an interest in how your partner spends his day, whether at work or at home, it strengthens your friendship. The challenge is to sustain interest in each other's lives while building new mutual interests at the same time. Valuing his beliefs and opinions, even when they are different from your own, produces an atmosphere of total honesty, where you can share all your thoughts and feelings.

To communicate honestly requires trust. You need to know that when you express your hopes and fears, your partner listens and values what you say without ridicule, rejection, or judgement. As you learn to communicate better, your level of trust and intimacy grows accordingly. Moving from one level of communication to another is a process that requires patience, understanding, encouragement, and diligence.

Having done everything to coexist peacefully, you still end up disagreeing now and then because, as we noted earlier, you are "two axes in one basket". What do you do when faced with conflict? I propose the following steps:

1. Identify and define the problem

Describe your problem in ways that seek a solution rather than prove that you have been wronged. Begin by explaining your own feelings, thoughts, and ideas, then allow your partner to do the same. As he goes about it, listen to him carefully, so that you may understand where he is coming from. Be an effective listener. "Everyone should be quick to listen, slow to speak, and slow to become angry." (James 1:19) When trying to resolve conflicts, rather than listening, we often tend to plan our responses before our spouse is done, be selective in our hearing, and be overly defensive. However, proper listening resolves differences by clarifying what our spouse is really feeling and saying.

Armed with both sides of the issue, seek a resolution that is satisfactory to both of you. It must be a win-win situation, where no one loses. Being honest about your own feelings, fears, and needs—and accepting and respecting your partner's own—is the most effective approach to conflict resolution.

2. Propose a variety of solutions

List down and discuss together different potential solutions that you both find acceptable. Out of these, settle on an immediate, amicable one. I say immediate because leaving the disagreement unresolved for long damages the relationship. Employ active listening techniques and respect your partner's ideas. Active listening is checking and confirming that you have actually understood your partner correctly by paraphrasing or summarising what he said.

3. Make a decision

A mutually acceptable agreement or solution is vital. The solution must be unambiguous, so that both parties understand it clearly. Do not try to persuade or pressure your partner into accepting a particular solution. Discuss and agree how to implement it. If one of you does not adhere to it, that person ought to be held accountable. Avoid nagging or constantly reminding your partner of his task; he already knows it. No one appreciates a nagging wife. Be willing to forgive, "[f]or if you forgive other people when they sin against you, your heavenly Father will also forgive you." (Matthew 6:14) Giving and receiving forgiveness is a nonnegotiable in resolving conflict with your spouse. Your ability to forgive your spouse will help both of you work towards achieving intimacy and a fulfilling, lasting marriage.

4. Evaluate

An evaluation after an agreed period is always helpful. The evaluation may reveal weaknesses in the original solution and necessitate revision or rethinking. In such a case, both parties should be willing to revise decisions; it should be done mutually, not by one party.

In closing, I reiterate that friendship in marriage is vitally important. The quality of a married couple's friendship is the most important predictor of fulfilling sex, romance, and passion. Love, respect, and compassion are all important elements of strong friendships. Practise positive sentiments towards each other. Good feelings for one another should always override the negative. It is easy for married partners to become experts at identifying each other's negative traits while ignoring or minimising positive ones. Negative sentiments are powerful and can destroy marriage and all other relationships.

Many relationship experts indicate that, in order to be happy in a marriage, it is important to give eight to 20 positive interactions for every negative one. Make a list of all the things you admire and appreciate about your spouse. Let him know what you like most and give affirmation from time to time. The next time you are tempted to focus on your partner's weakness, override it by focusing on the positive qualities you have already identified in him. Notice the good and generous things he does and express gratitude for them. Do not be overly critical; seek to be affirmative. Remember that your partner's strength may be your weakness and your strength, his weakness. Harness these deficient qualities and get the best out of them.

Friendship is a Journey

As we saw in an earlier chapter, it is easy to be friends during courtship and the early days of marriage. During this period, people tend to mask their real feelings; they do everything to avoid upsetting their loved one. Because of this, their hurt feelings may remain suppressed and hidden; after all, they are not so important. In most cases, some of the things that become major barriers and annoying habits are not new. We may have experienced them earlier, but they may have appeared inconsequential at that time. Disappointment, fear, shame, guilt, or rejection often erupts when our feel-good levels drop.

Friendship is a journey of learning and experience, of making mistakes and correcting them, of caring, communicating, committing to each other, and sharing common values. If the spark dies, then the couple need to understand that their relationship is being redefined. They can no longer sit long hours beside the fireplace, merely declaring their love for one another and enjoying each other's company. When responsibility sets in, it brings along work that has to be done. The fact that there are other things to attend to should not, in any way, mean that the friendship is under threat. It simply means that a new season has come and you have to respond to it. Enjoy the season!

Managing Attitudes, Self-Esteem, and Confidence

It is not your aptitude but your attitude,
[which] determines your altitude.
Zig Ziglar

C arl Rogers, in his book *On Becoming a Person*, talks about conditions of worth and their importance in the person. Self-esteem is the set of statements regarding the value that individuals put upon themselves—value in the sense of respect, admiration, pride, and enjoyment. The evaluation is an estimate of personal worth. The attitude and self-picture that we bring into our marriage determines if we find happiness and fulfilment in it. Self-esteem and self-confidence in ourselves is essential if we are to find satisfaction in any relationship. Self-esteem is the perception we have of ourselves. If it is positive, we then become self-confident.

Importance of Self-Esteem in Marriage

Before we get into a relationship, it is important to understand yourself—who you are, what makes you happy, and why you react to situations the way you do. Often the success of a relationship is determined by your attitudes and value system. Your self-concept affects how you think, how you perceive yourself, and how you behave. It also affects your relationship with significant others: your boyfriend, your husband, your friends, your children, and even your God. Self-concept is about how you perceive yourself: your ideal self, body image, self-image, and self-esteem. Each of the four elements is of equal importance. For most people, the core elements are firmly established; they interact harmoniously with each other. According to Rogers, the core elements must be mutually supportive; otherwise, the self-concept becomes dysfunctional.

A healthy and happy relationship should do your self-esteem much good, but if your self-esteem is not good to begin with, your partner cannot do much for you. He may do all he can to compliment and affirm you, but you find it hard to believe him. You tend to feel your partner is too good for you, and you are, therefore, not worthy of him. Such feelings can seriously damage a relationship. When you lack a realistic understanding of your abilities and strengths, you are unable to accept sincere compliments.

Njeri is a beautiful married young lady of 27, with one child. Although she is beautiful, she does not think so. She considers herself too fat and not tall enough. Her husband, who sincerely thinks she is beautiful, often compliments her. As she is overweight, though, she believes he only gives compliments to make her happy.

Njeri's husband, on the other hand, is a very attractive sanguine man, the life of the party, who often gets the attention of other women. In the beginning, Njeri was never bothered by the interest he received. Suddenly, she became conscious of it and even imagined him leaving her for someone more beautiful than herself.

Although Njeri's husband genuinely appreciates her, Njeri feels differently. Her problems arise from a low self-image; nothing her husband does can give her self-confidence. She says, "He is bothered by my behaviour and I feel terrible about it. I cannot explain what has happened to me and I am not able to change."

Emotional Abuse and Its Effects

Even in the midst of a disagreement, our choice of words is very important. It is always important to remember that you are not fighting an enemy, so avoid harsh, abusive language. People never forget hurtful words said to them. In the end, the relationship needs to be restored.

In a counselling session during one of my seminars, the group discussed the topic *Hurtful Words That Have Been Used against Me*. Participants relived hurtful words not only from their present relationships but also from childhood experiences. Some of the words were from their own parents.

- "You will not amount to anything; you are just like your mother."
- "You are so fat, I cannot stand you! Who would want you anyway?"
- "You dress like an old woman; your mother has better taste than you have."

- "I can never eat food you have prepared. You might have laced it with poison. After all, you want me to die, so that you can take my property."

Words spoken carelessly can be very damaging and negatively affect one's self-esteem and, consequently, the relationship. Do not use hurtful words to put down your spouse; they can wound him for life. Make a conscious effort to use words that build up rather than destroy; affirm rather than discourage. Discuss openly with your partner about issues that put you down or words that you would rather he did not use. On your part, if hurtful words have been used against you, you need to let go. God is a God of new beginnings; He will give you a clean, fresh start. Even if you have to go it alone, you will be amazed at the positive effect on your relationship.

In the earlier example, Njeri yearned for love, intimacy, and affection. She found the perfect partner who provided more than she had hoped for, but her inner insecurities remained. Now, their marriage was in trouble. Her low self-esteem slowly ate away at her marriage.

Njeri's marriage is not the only one in trouble. Purity, whose relationship is all but gone, cries, "Was I ever in love with this man? I guess I did not know him well enough because we dated for only a year. We hardly communicate. When we do, we fight over something. We no longer enjoy each other's company and are hardly intimate. I would rather you send me to the shamba for a long day's work than to sleep with my husband. Sex with him is boring. He is so selfish; all he cares about is himself. He never gives me money anymore and that is after he had depleted my finances. He asked me to leave my well-paid job to run a family business. Later, he decided I did not have the skill to manage it efficiently. **Never mind that I have a master's degree in business management and years of work experience. I now have to stay home. I drink myself to death. Please help me!"**

Where are you in your relationship? Maybe you were badly treated and psychologically abused before. People never said anything good about you; they made you feel worthless. They may have told you that you will never make a good wife or mother, which has deflated your confidence. You feel unable to move on because you cannot even believe in yourself. Perhaps, you feel it is just a matter of time before your husband rejects you in favour of someone more beautiful and more worthy of the honour.

Do not let low self-esteem ruin your relationship. You must get up and move on! You have no alternative but to work on your self-esteem, so you can realise your true value and experience your partner's love and respect. You have to bring yourself to the place where you believe that it is right and prudent for them to love you and be positive towards you.

Low self-esteem makes you defensive because you always expect to be criticised. It can present itself as oversensitivity. When you are overly sensitive, you become defensive and are always ready to pick a fight. You feel that other people are always about to attack you, so you have to protect yourself. Others may withdraw into their shell and let the world pass them by.

People with low self-esteem often describe themselves as unlovable. They have a bad attitude and attitude influences what we attract. What we attract eventually determines what we become. People always outwardly project what they feel inside.

Attitude is a picture of who we are inside, so it is important to adopt a positive attitude towards your relationship. The Bible reminds us that "as [you] think within [yourself], so [you are]" (Proverbs 23:7). Say to yourself, "I am good. I am wonderful. I am a great person. I deserve nothing but the best, which is why God gives me every good and perfect gift. I have a great husband, friend, and companion. I have a good marriage, great friends and an assured future, even if things do not seem that way now."

Remember that you are a daughter of the Heavenly Father; you are fearfully and wonderfully created in His image. Honour Him by boldly standing up as His princess! As Marianne Williamson, a spiritual activist, author, and lecturer, says, "Our deepest fear is not that we are inadequate. Our deepest fear is that we are powerful beyond measure. It is our light, not our darkness, that most frightens us."

A lady once said to me, "I gave up on my marriage a long time ago. Our eight years of marriage went down the drain; my husband does not exist in my books anymore. We share the house because I will not move out, but he can leave if he chooses to do so. He is dead as far as I am concerned. What he does is his business and what I do has nothing to do with him." My heart bled for this girl. Although what she said sounded confident and final, I read it differently. What I heard was a desperate cry for help, so I engaged her in conversation and encouraged her to talk about their happier days: their courtship, their children, and her husband's most likable characteristics. By the end of our conversation, she had lit up and was willing to seek counsel to save her marriage. Her attitude had changed.

Do not dwell on the weakness of your partner, but enjoy and celebrate his strengths. You may be very strong where he is weak, so you complement one another. It is for that very reason that the Lord promised him a helper.

So how do you build up or rebuild your self-esteem? Here are some useful thoughts:

1. Accept your body image

Our body size and structure is not just a reflection of our eating and exercise habits, it is also that of our genetics. A tall, slim body may be the dream of many ladies, but not everyone is meant to be a fashion model. Our body image—how we think, feel, or react to our physical attributes—greatly influences our self-image. Learn to dress well to flatter your body shape, but remember Paul's admonition in 1 Timothy 2:9-10: "I also want the women to dress modestly, with decency and propriety, adorning themselves, not with elaborate hairstyles or gold or pearls or expensive clothes, but with good deeds, appropriate for women who profess to worship God."

We can enhance our body image because it is not fixed. It changes as we grow older and each stage in our life is associated with a body image change. Building a positive body image is a lifelong process. It is more than changing our body; it means changing how we feel, think, and react to our body size or form. We may be unable to make ourselves thin, but that should not stop us from being healthy in body and mind, regardless of our size or society's expectations. When we have a positive body image, we value and respect our body.

So accept your body image and celebrate your uniqueness. Remember: "Beauty is in the eye of the beholder."

2. Talk positively about yourself

What we say about ourselves is very important. Listen to what you say to and about yourself. We always have mental dialogues with ourselves. Do you constantly put yourself down? Do you call yourself names? It would be helpful to list down your achievements. Acknowledging them affirms your value and worth. You might just find out that you have achieved much more than you realise, which can boost your self-esteem. Remind yourself often that you are special, created in the image and likeness of God (Genesis 1:26).

3. Surround yourself with positive friends

Blessed is the one who does not walk in step with the wicked...
(Psalm 1:1a)

Spend time with people who value you, who affirm and encourage you, and bring out your very best. Friends are important people in our lives, but I have learned that not every friend is good. This understanding comes with maturity. If someone constantly puts you down and criticises you, if someone never acknowledges your strengths but always points out your weaknesses, you can do well without them. If a relationship takes up your energy and always has a negative effect on you, maybe it is time to move on. Make other friends who add value to your life. The people you choose to hang out with often reflect how you feel about yourself. Friends sharpen each other as iron sharpens iron. True friends can keep you sharp in every way. They let you know when you go too far off track and help you get through and make sense of life's challenges. "As iron sharpens iron, so one person sharpens another." (Proverbs 27:17)

4. Be gentle to yourself

You can only attract people and circumstances that match the quality and intensity of your beliefs and values, which is why being gentle with yourself is vital. You can visualise and affirm all you want, but if you feel unworthy in your heart, you can forget receiving anything. We often tend to be too impatient with ourselves, while, at the same time, we weigh ourselves down with unrealistic expectations. Be patient with yourself and others as well; nobody is perfect! When you make a mistake, accept it as that and move on. Dwelling on your mistakes stunts your development. Criticising yourself, beating yourself up, feeling sorry for yourself, and being disappointed in your own behaviour is not virtuous, honourable, or productive in any way.

It does not matter how long you have carried your bad attitude; it is never too late to change. The choice is yours. Yesterday is gone, but today is here and tomorrow is coming. You have a lifetime ahead of you. Make good use of the gifts God so graciously gave you, even if you do not have your dream physique or you have quite a few weaknesses. Learn to have a positive attitude towards yourself. In 2 Corinthians 12:1-10, Paul cries out about "a thorn in [his] flesh", which tormented him. Many times, he asked God to remove it, but the Lord chose instead to give him the grace to bear his condition, to live with his pain, flaw, or hardship. Whatever the thorn in the flesh was, Paul acknowledged that God's grace was sufficient for him to accept and live with the circumstances.

Whatever your struggles, rest assured that if you call upon God, He gives you victory over the situation. "Call to me and I will answer you..." (Jeremiah 33:3) and "[I will] do immeasurably more than all [you] ask or imagine..." (Ephesians 3:20), the Lord says in the Bible. He can take it away or give you the strength to live with or even profit from a negative situation.

5. Give yourself a treat

One of the best ways to improve your self-esteem is to do something for yourself, which affirms you. Buy yourself a new dress. Get a new hairstyle. Have a facial, massage, pedicure, and/or manicure. Work out at the gym. Run 10 kilometres every day. Whatever it is, do something that lifts you up. Your self-image has been affected by many influences and in different ways. You may even be unaware of how much they have affected your thoughts about yourself. It is time for you, a child of God, to take up your rightful place and to maintain a healthy self-image.

6. Understand personality differences

No two people are born with the same personality. I have had the privilege of giving birth to and raising twins. Born on the same day and same hour and brought up in the same environment by the same parents, they are still very different from each other. Their difference is a blessing for me and my family because each of them brings unique gifts. As a family, we are favoured to enjoy their different strengths, talents, and abilities. In all, I have brought up three biological children and no two of them are alike.

I had different expectations as a young mother; I expected them to be very similar. I remember shouting at one or the other in exasperation, "Can you not be like your sister?" One of my daughters always took great offence whenever I said this. To this day, she continues to remind me that she never liked it. Regrettably, I did not know better at that time. Today, I celebrate their uniqueness.

When I married Bob, I also had expectations of what a husband should be and how he ought to behave and treat me and our children. I was in for a rude shock. He already had his established and set ways and was not about to fit into my idea of a model husband. I had read too many Mills & Boon novels; I had many fantasies in my mind. I expected Bob to hold my hand as we walked, open the car door for me, and, of course, call me "darling". How wrong I was!

Finally, your esteem can receive a great boost, if you understand the uniqueness of your position as a woman and a wife. A woman has a special calling in the ministry of the home. God has appointed and anointed you to turn your home into something beautiful.

Life always presents us with problems and challenges because God never promised us one without pain. The best we can do is to change our attitude towards them as they come our way. An acronym that helps me cope comes from one of John Maxwell's writings from which I have learnt a great deal:

PROBLEMS

Predictors	They help mould our future.
Reminders	We are not self-sufficient; we need God and others for help.
Opportunities	They pull us out of our rut and cause us to think creatively.
Blessings	They open up doors that are normally unavailable for us to enter.
Lessons	Each new challenge will be our teacher.
Everywhere	No place or person is excluded from them.
Messages	They warn us about potential disasters.
Solvable	No problem is without a solution.

The Bible reminds us that character is developed only through challenges. It is only through trials that our faith is strengthened and our character developed (James1:2-4). The next time you go through a difficult situation, receive it as an opportunity to learn, to grow, and to glow.

Our attitude determines whether our relationship works or not. If we get into a relationship halfheartedly and without commitment, it will not work. That is why come-we-stay marriages never work because the people involved have not committed themselves to the relationship.

How is your attitude today? Keep smiling and stay positive!

Chapter Five

Intimacy and the Marriage Bed

*Marriage should be honoured by all, and the
marriage bed kept pure...*
Hebrews 13:4

The marriage bed must be a place of mutuality: the husband seeking to satisfy his wife, the wife seeking to satisfy her husband. Marriage is not a place to stand up for your rights. There must be a conscious decision to serve the other, whether in or out of bed. It says in 1 Corinthians 7:3-5: "The husband should fulfil his marital duty to his wife, and likewise the wife to her husband. The wife does not have authority over her own body but yields it to her husband. In the same way, the husband does not have authority over his own body but yields it to his wife. Do not deprive each other except perhaps by mutual consent and for a time, so that you may devote yourselves to prayer. Then come together again so that Satan will not tempt you because of your lack of self-control."

Maintaining Intimacy

Intimacy is the closeness, oneness, and togetherness between you and your partner. Marriage and family researchers Mark Schaefer and David Olson describe it as "a process that occurs over time and is never completed or fully accomplished". Development of intimacy is a journey that lasts throughout your married life. It is experienced emotionally, spiritually, intellectually, sexually, and in many other ways. In another book by Olson and coauthored by Amy Olson, they assert that "married people tend to be healthier, live longer, have more wealth and economic assets, and have more satisfying sexual relationships". Mental health is also better for couples with healthy intimacy. Researchers Robert Firestone and Joyce Catlett say, "In our opinion, love is the one force that is capable of easing depression".

Characteristics of Intimacy

Relationships that experience healthy intimacy have several factors in common, including the following.

1. Mutual trust

Trust is crucial in all relationships and particularly in building an intimate relationship with your spouse. It is cultivated and nurtured over long periods and can be destroyed in a very short time. It is a powerful tool that helps the relationship grown in every aspect.

This builds a sense of security for both you and your spouse. You can show it by never hurting your spouse in any way. Though you might unintentionally cause hurt, you should not hurt one another on purpose. Be gentle in your expressions of caring. Without trust, couples cannot enjoy intimacy. They grow distant, suspicious, angry, bitter, and resentful.

2. Acceptance

Acceptance is key to enjoying a healthy and happy marriage. It is not easy for two people of completely different backgrounds to come together and share a home and a life of being one. It requires compromise and unconditional acceptance. Accept your spouse as he is and do not lose your energies in trying to change him. You may be bothered by your spouse's habits or idiosyncrasies; it may take a while for him to change.

> *Intimacy is the closeness, oneness, and togetherness between you and your partner.*

No one is perfect, but acceptance means not holding weaknesses against each other. If you find yourself frequently pointing out your spouse's faults, then focus instead on his qualities that made you fall in love with him in the first place. Accept your circumstances regardless of the situation, for marriage does not guarantee you a smooth ride after the vows. Life sometimes has a way of handing us surprises that we least expect. In spite of what happens, remember your commitment to the relationship and your vow: for richer or poorer, better or worse, in sickness and in health. There are times that life presents you a storm and all you can do is fight it or go with the flow, making the most of it. Accept the circumstances, brace yourself, and move forward.

3. Open communication

Communication is the foundation from which a strong marital union grows. It is absolutely vital that couples learn how to have an open and honest communication, if they want to have a successful, happy, and lasting marriage. Communicate in many different ways, not just verbal but also nonverbal. Communication (the ability to discuss anything with your spouse) includes sincere expression of thoughts and feelings, as well as careful listening. Signs of poor communication include reluctance to tell your spouse about the events of your day or unwillingness to listen when your spouse explains his feelings.

Understanding what your spouse wants to hear comes by listening to them and understanding their personality. It is also important to give your spouse clues about what you need. Do not assume that he will understand what you mean; you have to tell him. If you need or want something, tell your spouse. Do not take for granted that he will be able to guess things on his own.

Many relationships fail because of misunderstanding and open communication skills are necessary if your relationship is to stay strong. If you sense that your spouse is disconnected or you are unhappy about something, do not ignore or turn a blind eye to the situation. Suggest an open discussion to iron out the issues. You may be frustrated, angry, or hurt, and he may be, too. Your goal should be to resolve the differences, and the only viable way of doing so is through open and direct communication.

4. Caring

This is genuine concern for your spouse's well-being. Often, we underestimate the power of a smile, a kind gesture, and the act of caring. If you do things you know hurt your spouse, then you cannot have healthy intimacy. You can develop a more caring heart and mind by considering your spouse's feelings before your own. Always ask yourself before acting or speaking: "If I do this or say this, will I hurt my partner?"

5. Apologising

Apologies are the remedy for mistakes that spouses inevitably make. Recognising mistakes, taking responsibility for them, expressing remorse for any hurt caused, and committing to change the hurtful behaviour are all essential to mending the relationship. For spouses who have created a chasm of hurts that separates them, a sincere and humble apology is the first step towards building a bridge across the gap. Even if you believe that your partner made the mistake, you can trigger the healing process by finding something you did that calls for an apology.

6. Forgiveness

Forgiveness is the process of letting go of anger, of a desire for revenge, and of an obsessive recollection of times your spouse has hurt you. It includes allowing your spouse to have weaknesses, make mistakes, and change. Seeing the goodness and strengths of your spouse along with his weaknesses can open up emotional space for goodwill to develop between the two of you. Forgiveness does not automatically create trust or reconciliation nor does it mean approval of bad behaviour. It is, however, an important early step towards rebuilding a fractured relationship.

7. Boundaries

Appropriate boundaries are the limits you place on a relationship. The limits can be set individually or together as a couple. These limits include saying "no" when your spouse asks you to do something that goes against your values or is more than you can handle. Setting firm, clear boundaries for yourself and respecting the boundaries of your partner create feelings of safety and trust. Healthy intimacy comprises pursuing your own interests independent of your spouse's and encouraging him to do the same. Your respective pursuits should not get in the way of building intimacy; it should not involve inappropriate relationships with your spouse. Spending reasonable time on personal interests helps each partner be happier and a more interesting and well-rounded companion.

Intimacy is an important part of a vibrant, loving marriage.

Intimacy is an important part of a vibrant, loving marriage. It can be experienced at many levels, including physical, emotional, spiritual, mental, financial, and recreational. Intimacy is nurtured through mutual trust, tenderness, acceptance, open communication, caring, apologising, forgiveness, and boundaries. Couples can work together to increase their intimacy in each area, as they build their marriage through the years.

Types of Intimacy

The term intimacy can mean different things to different people and at different stages of marriage. Let us look at the following types of intimacy.

1. Emotional intimacy

This is the closeness created through shared feelings. Growing up, my sisters and I were allowed to show our emotions freely. It was, however, different for my brothers. They were told that real men are not allowed to express their emotions openly. When they showed their feelings, they were reminded that they were men and should not cry or behave like women. I never once saw my father shed a tear or show any emotion in whatever circumstances. Do not worry if your husband never shows his emotions; it may have to do with his socialisation rather than his feelings about you. There is hope. Even if he never learnt how to be emotionally intimate while growing up, he can learn it as an adult.

The first step towards emotional awareness and expression is to look out for your feelings, identify them, and think of possible reasons for them. Notice the differences between strong emotions, such as terror and fury, and subtle emotions, such as anxiety, insecurity, and irritation. Emotional intimacy can only occur once people know what they feel, how to convey feelings to each other, and how to express concern and understanding of feelings towards each other.

2. Spiritual intimacy

This involves sharing and observing religious beliefs and practices together, such as praying and attending church. Praying together with my husband has been a great point of intimacy. No matter how angry I may be, the pain has a way of melting away when we pray together. It gives us a chance to start on a clean slate. If God forgives us and promises us His mercy, how much more should we forgive the one we love so dearly?

As you share spiritual experiences, you become united in your attitudes and goals. Ed Wheat, a medical doctor and "certified sex therapist", suggests that couples should become active in church, where they can serve God, learn, and grow together, alongside others. If you and your spouse struggle with incompatible religious beliefs, then seek help. The Bible observes that two cannot walk together unless they agree.

3. Recreational intimacy

This involves enjoying activities together, such as working out or playing a sport. Bob and I play golf together and it is simply wonderful; we always look forward to those moments. We not only enjoy the game, but we also use the time to bond. In the early days of our marriage, I always stayed at home whenever he took part in his favourite sports. Bob was passionate about tennis and squash, and loved jogging. As for me, I was too busy bringing up our children, running our business, and managing the home. I was not passionate about sporting activities, as I was already overwhelmed with my responsibilities. Besides, I was not at all interested in his interests. Many times, I questioned them. Although I am his wife, I felt at that time that I ranked far below his precious games.

Once I finally joined him in a game, I never looked back. Playing together gives us an opportunity to do something we both enjoy, while spending quality time together. Get involved in your husband's recreational activities as long as the family does not suffer in your absence. During our marriage fitness sessions with men, most of them complain that their wives are not interested in them, their work, or their hobbies. I recall a man complaining, "Before we got married, my wife and I did everything together. She never minded going out with me, regardless of what I did or where I went. She had a way of turning everything into fun. Now everything has changed. She is simply not the woman I married; she is engrossed in her life and cares little about me."

No doubt your new role as wife and, perhaps, mother can be overwhelming. I often felt the same way; however, no matter how much you have to do, remember to take care of your partner, too. Get involved; take an interest in his life, even if it entails just listening to his description of how he did himself proud!

4. Sexual intimacy

Sex is a vital component of marriage, so it is one of the most important dimensions of a healthy marital intimacy. Healthy sexual intimacy includes frequency, satisfaction, variety of sexual activities both partners enjoy, and openness to talk freely about sex. Olson and Olson observe that "a major strength for happily married couples is the quality of the sexual relationship". In their research, they discovered that the most common sexual concern among couples is varying levels of interest in sex. They concluded that happy couples tend to agree in their definition of sexual satisfaction. They have fewer worries about their sex lives than unhappy couples have. They noted that more than half of all married couples have trouble discussing sexual issues.

Sexual desires are a normal part of our humanity. If you are a normal, functioning person, it should not surprise you when you find yourself physically attracted to someone or sexually aroused. God made every one of us a sexual being and still found the work of His hands good! Attraction and arousal are the natural, spontaneous responses to physical beauty; anybody with fully functional senses ought to acknowledge that.

Sexual energy and compatibility often play a big role in the first phase of a relationship. As time goes on, however, other factors, such as honesty, trust, and mutual respect become increasingly more important. As part of the blessing of marriage, God gives us the pleasure of showing love through physical union and the open display of mutual affection, all within the bounds of a secure relationship. The physical union in marriage is intended not only for procreation but also for pleasure.

God is the Creator of every good and perfect gift, including sexual expression. The Bible wonderfully emphasises the value and goodness of sex in our lives in both Old and New Testaments. It handles this subject in a very wholesome way. Human sexuality is expressed in marriage and is, above all, spiritually edifying.

For the newlywed with no experience of lovemaking: Sex is natural, so relax and enjoy yourself, when the time comes. These days, we have various speakers in bridal showers, who give details to the bride and her peers on "sex techniques". Listening to some of the advice given, I wonder what sex is really all about. One thing I can confidently say is that, although emphasis is given to the physical aspect of the relationship, there is so much more to sex than the physical. It involves emotions, too—a connection that grows with time, creating a magical oneness.

Often there is a tendency to overdramatise sex; it has much coverage prior to marriage. There are various opinions as to how prepared a bride should be for sex in marriage. Most of them are based on culture and values. A friend shared with me about her culture concerning sex: The aunties prepare the girl for marriage. They accompany her after the wedding and remain in her matrimonial home for one week, training her on the dos and don'ts of marriage.

Because of the nature of the relationship and youthful energies, sex is spontaneous. Learning techniques prior to marriage relationship would not be my option. At a bridal shower I facilitated, I spoke on friendship, intimacy, and oneness in marriage. Then the mother of the bride asked me to expound on the physical aspect of sex. The bride blushed. I did not want to take that direction especially because this was a forum of mothers and daughters. I understood where she came from, though, because it has become the norm for speakers at bridal showers to give details on techniques. As I said earlier, sex is natural, so creativity should be encouraged. It is never the same for any two people.

Sexual intimacy is important to a woman and every woman likes and craves to be touched. A speaker on the love languages emphasised the woman's need for touch. Unless she is touched eight times a day, she cannot be joyful – with the eighth touch being the sexual act itself. The nature of a woman requires and requests that she is touched, caressed, embraced, and admired. God wired the woman that way. Sexual intimacy goes a long way in the way their husbands affirm them. When a woman is sexually fulfilled, she is on top of the world and is madly in love with her husband.

God wants us to be madly in love with our husbands. He wants us to keep the fire burning in our marriage beds! As you and your partner grow and develop, each of you will change with time. If you cannot find common ground as you grow individually, you may find yourselves becoming strangers while living in the same house, especially if you encounter challenges. With issues of sexual intimacy in marriage, where do you go? The answer is in God's word.

The Song of Songs is a perfect example of a God-honouring union between two people obviously intoxicated with each other. Here are some verses from the book that is also sometimes called the Song of Solomon:

How beautiful your
sandalled feet,
O prince's daughter!
Your graceful legs
are like jewels,
the work of an
artist's hands.
Your navel is a
rounded goblet that
never lacks blended wine.
Your waist is a mound
of wheat encircled by lilies.
Your breasts are
like two fawns,
like twin fawns of a gazelle. Your neck is like an ivory tower. Your
eyes are the pools of Heshbon by the gate of Bath Rabbim.
(7:1-4a)

How beautiful you are and how pleasing, my love, with your
delights! Your stature is like that of the palm, and your breasts like
clusters of fruit.
(7:6-7)

> *I belong to my beloved, and his desire is for me. Come, my beloved, let us go to the countryside, let us spend the night in the villages. Let us go early to the vineyards to see if the vines have budded, if their blossoms have opened, and if the pomegranates are in bloom—there I will give you my love.*
> (7:10-12)

I encourage you and your spouse to go through the entire Song of Songs together; you will not only be inspired but also learn good love songs and poems to sing to one another.

God's Intention for Sex

God's plan for sex is good, pleasing, and perfect; it is not only for procreation but also for pleasure, joy, and expressing love. In marriage, each person should regard their bodies as belonging to their mate (1 Corinthians 7:4). You only refrain from sex with each other by mutual agreement, such as in times of fasting (verse 5). Aside from the above, the Bible does not put further restrictions on how a married couple engage in sex.

Not in the Mood

When you are not in the mood for sex, there could be many reasons: fatigue, boredom, and low testosterone – the male hormone that experts suspect contributes to a woman's sexual drive. Other factors could be a new baby and, generally, your new role as wife, mother, provider, etc. Once the honeymoon stage in marriage is over, new responsibilities may send sex farther down the wife's priority list, as she grapples with the challenges. On the other hand, the husband may be so preoccupied with excelling in his career and dealing with other stresses in his life that he cannot give his wife due attention. This does not change the fact that they have a responsibility to meet each other's needs, sexual needs included.

It is important to note that sex rates very highly in a man's needs. Willard Harley, in his book *His Needs, Her Needs*, rates sexual satisfaction as number one priority for men, while affection is the first priority for a woman. Other needs of men cited are companionship in leisure time, an attractive woman, a tidy home, and admiration, in that order. For the woman, it is conversation, trust, security, and his participation in the family life.

When one partner loses interest in sex for one reason or another, it is important not to judge them; instead, openly discuss the issue. Women generally avoid sex when they are angry with their partners. They use sex as a weapon to fight their partners or to retaliate. At one moment in Kenya, some nongovernmental organisations called for a seven-day sex boycott by women to press their husbands to act in support of political reforms. It generated a huge debate. One thing, however, is certain: Sex is not a tool or weapon for fighting.

Communication, financial issues, and suspicion of infidelity are some other reasons why a woman fakes a headache when, in reality, she is upset and annoyed and not ready to submit her body to the man. Let your partner know that you are angry and hurt but willing to sort out the issue. When you use sex as a weapon to fight your partner, you worsen the situation and leave the problem unresolved. Do not criticise your husband. If you do, you damage his ego and he may not respond to you after that.

Sexual failures, incompatibilities, or indiscretions provide some of the major challenges that face marriage. Some women have confessed to living in sexless marriages for years. Others complain of sexual boredom and lack of passion. Many view marital sex as dull, boring, and always predictable. Difficulties of the everyday family life do not help either. During one marriage fitness seminar, I opened up a discussion on the topic, which generated much debate. Below are samples of what some people had to say on the subject:

"Sex is a huge issue in my marriage because my husband wants it all the time. I am often not in the mood and, at such times, I just cannot get myself to do it. Not long ago, he asked me to tell him what I like in bed. Although it really is not a big deal for me, I suggested something I wanted us to try. Since then, he accused me of having an affair. He claimed that since I did not learn lovemaking that way from him, I must have picked it up from someone else. He later apologised, but I am still offended. It has been six months since we were last intimate. I am thinking of leaving him, if things do not get better."

"I have come to hate it so much; I actually have to take a shower afterwards, when it happens. I feel abused. Sex used to be great, but it is now outdated. For me, it is just his way of relieving himself. There is no longer any petting, any kind words, just penetration. Before long, it is over and he then snores away."

"I am so busy with the children, tired from my full-time job, and sometimes frustrated with so many responsibilities that sex is the last thing on my mind."

"I give up on my husband. He comes home from work and just sits, either reading the newspaper or watching the news. He does not notice me all evening. I always go to bed before him because he carries work home. And just when I begin enjoying

my sleep, he creeps into bed, expecting sex! I simply feel put off."

Talking about sex and the needs of each partner in an open and candid way is important for couples to enjoy a fulfilling sexual relationship. Friendship, trust, and good communication play a major role in enhancing the sexual relationship and, consequently, help ensure a lasting marriage.

Infidelity

One cannot talk about sexual intimacy without including the issue of infidelity. Infidelity is not always sexual; many times, there is emotional infidelity in relationships. Energy, time, and money can be spent on someone else whom you see more often than you should. Such relationships are often justified because a sexual relationship does not exist within the marriage. Infidelity can also be risky to the entire family, when one partner handles finances irresponsibly.

Marriage has its challenges, but few compare to the monumental task of healing from infidelity. As a marriage counsellor, I have heard clients confess that the discovery of an affair was the lowest, darkest moment of their entire lives. Because affairs shatter trust, many seriously contemplate an end to their marriage and even to their own lives. However, know that no matter how bleak things might seem, it is possible to revitalise a marriage wounded by infidelity. It is not easy, but years of experience have taught me that there are definite patterns for bringing marriages back from the brink of disaster.

In 1 Corinthians 7:28b, Paul warns, "But those who marry will face many troubles in this life". To give us hope, Jesus says, "I have told you these things, so that in me you may have peace. In this world you will have trouble. But take heart! I have overcome the world." (John 16:33)

Marriage brings together two people who are not perfect. From a fallen and sinful world, both bring with them good and bad traits, habits, sins, and selfish desires. Both are like sheep gone astray, but they want to be happy. Jesus comforts us that even though we will have trouble, there is a solution.

Healing from infidelity involves teamwork; both spouses

> *Healing from infidelity involves teamwork; both spouses must be fully committed to the hard work of putting their marriage back on track.*

must be fully committed to the hard work of putting their marriage back on track. The unfaithful partner must end the affair and do whatever it takes to win back the trust of the other spouse. The betrayed spouse must find ways to manage the overwhelming emotions. More importantly, both need to establish mechanisms to ensure that it never happens again. No two people, marriages, or paths to recovery are identical, but know that healing typically happens in stages.

If you have recently discovered that your spouse has been unfaithful, you undoubtedly feel a whole range of emotions: shock, rage, hurt, devastation, disillusionment, and despair. You may have difficulty sleeping or eating, or feel completely obsessed with the affair. If you are an emotional person, you may cry a lot. You may want to be alone or, conversely, feel at your worst when you are. While unpleasant, these reactions are perfectly normal.

Although you may tell yourself that your marriage will never recover, it will but not immediately. Healing from infidelity takes time—sometimes, a long time. Just when you think things are better, something reminds you of the affair and you rapidly go downhill. It is easy to feel discouraged, unless you both keep in mind that intense difficulties are part of the process. In time, the setbacks will be fewer and farther in between, moving the process faster.

Some people are more curious than others, so it is common to have many questions about the affair, especially at the beginning. If you have little interest in the facts, so be it; however, if you need to know what happened, ask. Although the details may be uncomfortable to hear, your spouse's willingness to "come clean" should help your recovery, as it does for some people. As the unfaithful spouse, you may feel tremendous remorse and guilt and, therefore, prefer not to revisit the details. Experience shows that this is a formula for disaster. Hiding negative feelings and persistent questions make genuine healing unlikely.

Once what actually happened is disclosed, there is typically a need to know why it happened. Betrayed spouses often believe that, unless they find the underlying cause, it could occur again. Unfortunately, because reasons for infidelity can be quite complex, the "whys" are not always clear.

The reasons for marital infidelity vary greatly from one person to the other. Many times, an affair is never the cause of a broken marriage, but it brings with it others factors that cause the marriage to eventually break down. Generally, after many years of marriage, partners can grow too familiar with each other, which is inevitable. Often, I have heard it argued that an affair will make you a better lover, a better person, help you with your self-esteem and improve your relationships—not to mention the vigour it will give you during your midlife crisis. Other people allege that it will inevitably bring joy, pleasure, and excitement back into your marriage. Forget it! That is an illusion. An affair might temporarily give you more sex, a great thrill, and a feeling of ecstasy, but it could also cause an irreparable damage or even bring your marriage to an end. It may make it impossible to live with your once Prince Charming—your beloved husband, your children, and family. Is it worth it?

Some other known reasons for extramarital affairs include conflict or intimacy avoidance, sexual deprivation or addiction, and revenge. It can also involve self-esteem issues, where one seeks physical validation, or emotional issues, when one did not marry the love of her life. Some spouses succumb to the lure of an extramarital relationship as a result of experiencing abnormal stress over a normal lifestyle change, such as becoming a parent or during the empty-nest period. It happens that adultery can occur in both happy and unhappy marriages. It is painful that, while one partner may be strictly faithful in the marriage, the other may be swayed and led into infidelity for reasons unrelated to what the other partner does or does not do.

Still, it is important to note that infidelity is a choice, a decision that one makes. No one can force another to be unfaithful. If you have been unfaithful, examine why you allowed yourself to do something that threatens your marriage, and seek help. If your partner continues to be adulterous, the situation must be addressed as soon as possible. Infidelity must not be allowed to continue unchecked.

It is equally important to explore if your marriage has significant shortcomings in some areas. No marriage is perfect, but people sometimes feel so unhappy that they look to others for a stronger emotional or physical connection. They complain of being taken for granted, unloved, resented, or ignored. It could also be a lack of general or sexual intimacy in the marriage.

If unhappiness with your spouse contributed to your infidelity, you need to address your feelings openly and honestly, so that you can make changes together. If open communication is a problem, seek help from qualified marital therapists. Many are available through religious organisations, community colleges, and mental health facilities. While honest discussions are important, they are not the only thing to do. Couples who successfully rebuild their marriages recognise the importance of spending time together, talking about their difficulties without dwelling on painful topics. They intentionally create opportunities to reconnect and nurture their friendship.

Ultimately, the key to healing from infidelity is forgiveness, which is often the last step in the healing process. The unfaithful spouse can do everything right—be forthcoming with confession, express remorse, listen lovingly, and act honourably, but the marriage will still not mend, unless the betrayed person forgives the unfaithful spouse. The offending partner must also learn to forgive themselves. Forgiveness reopens the door to true intimacy and connection, but it will not just happen by itself. It results from a conscious decision to stop the blame game, make peace, and start anew on a clean slate. If the past has had you in its clutches, take the next step to have more love in your life: Decide to forgive today.

"How can I ever trust again?" is one of the most commonly asked questions, when there has been infidelity in a marriage. Nothing has the capacity to cause more destruction in a marital relationship than that which relates to sexual impurity. No wonder God's word admonishes us to keep the matrimonial bed pure (Hebrews 13:4).

Dazed by the reality of her husband's infidelity, Marilyn asked, "How can I move on after my beloved husband cheated on me? I really want to move on and spend the rest of my life with him, take care of our children together, and grow old together, but my heart bleeds. I feel so hurt and rejected. There seems to be a constant battle between my mind and my heart. I struggle because we committed to our marriage, to being faithful to one another. We have done well and I trusted him because he had proven trustworthy, dependable, and honest. Now that he has gone behind my back with my girlfriend, I am hurting. What will happen after this? Is there life after infidelity? Can we really have a marriage?"

Yes, you can, Marilyn. You can have a fulfilling, lasting marriage, if you decide to forgive and do it. Commit to what brought you together in the first place. Move towards healing and recovery, with God's help.

While sex is perfectly holy and pure within marriage, it is forbidden outside of it by the Lord. The world, however, does not recognise or honour this distinction. Consequently, its God-intended holiness and purity is destroyed. A slackening of God's standard, where sexual relationships happen wherever and with whomever one chooses, brings only guilt and misery.

In all our relationships with the opposite sex, we must make a clear and positive stand against this attitude. It saves us from being trapped and is a clear testimony to the world. We must clearly state that sex is only intended by God for one man and one woman, within the confines of marriage. Let us, therefore, keep our bodies—the temple of the Holy Spirit—pure and private, until He gives us a marriage partner with whom this holy relationship and our physical desires can be satisfied.

Sexual behaviour is determined by values rather than knowledge. Generally, men who become adulterous do not begin their errant ways after marriage; they begin earlier. When I asked Marilyn about her husband's fidelity before marriage, she told me that he dated two other girls, while they were already seeing each other. She did not mind it at that time, but now that she had him, she was offended when he went out with other women. Listen: Marriage does not guarantee behaviour change. You may want to believe that your boyfriend will change when he marries you, but you should forget it. You are lying only to yourself.

Our beliefs and values play a major role in our character. Some of the most significant values that shape our sexual character are chastity, integrity, respect for self and others, and responsibility. We do not imbibe them overnight, nor are they burnt into our hearts at the altar when we say "I do"; they are formed in us along the journey of life.

Affairs usually begin with an attraction to someone you know fairly well, someone you spend time with, say, a friend or a co-worker. The source of Marilyn's greatest pain is that her husband had his affair with her girlfriend Chebet. Looking back, Marilyn admits that she lived in denial for too long and should have suspected that the two were up to no good.

We Are All Vulnerable

It is helpful to understand that, under certain conditions, we are all capable of infidelity. What is important is to know when to flee (2 Timothy 2:22). Lust is an act of the will. Sexual temptation always begins in the mind, not in circumstances. Jesus said, "For it is from within, out of a person's heart, that evil thoughts come—sexual immorality, theft, murder, adultery, greed, malice, deceit, lewdness, envy, slander, arrogance, and folly. All these evils come from inside and defile a person." (Mark 7:21-23)

Paul's warning to Christians is clear: "Do not be deceived: Neither the sexually immoral nor idolaters nor adulterers nor men who have sex with men nor thieves nor the greedy nor drunkards nor slanderers nor swindlers will inherit the kingdom of God." (1 Corinthians 6:9b-10) Faced with the current attitudes of the world to these things, you must ensure that your standards are not lowered. The old nature within us should not be allowed to express itself and make us prey to temptations.

God instituted the institution of marriage and sanctified it. In the same way, He commands all people to keep it holy and to keep away from all things such as adultery and marital unfaithfulness that may destroy that foundational relationship. His command is clear and unequivocal: "Marriage should be honoured by all, and the marriage bed kept pure, for God will judge the adulterer and all the sexually immoral." (Hebrews 13:4)

The Lord, who is the author and finisher of our faith, can help you keep your marriage pure and wholesome, according to His will, if only you ask Him and do as He says.

The following are pitfalls to avoid:

1. Do not openly criticise your husband.

2. Keep the channels of communication open.

3. Do not deny sex to your husband, without good reason.

4. Keep the home fire burning; pray for one another.

5. Do not discuss your sex life with others.

Chapter Six

Marriage as God Intended: The Biblical Basis of Marriage

*That is why a man leaves his father
and mother and is united to his wife,
and they become one flesh.*
Genesis 2:24

Marriage is permanently sealed by a covenant and physically consummated in sexual union. It is God's design for two to become one flesh. This aspect fulfils three important elements of the marriage relationship: to produce children (Genesis 1:28), to eliminate solitude (Genesis 2:18), and to have physical fulfilment (1 Corinthians 7:2).

The sexual relationship cannot be compartmentalised; it affects the rest of the marriage. In *The Marriage Book*, Nicky and Sila Lee observe that, whereas sex may not be the icing on the cake, it is still a vital ingredient of the cake itself. Without sex, a husband and wife are just housemates, when they are supposed to be lovers.

Cleaving is a litmus test for couples to determine their detachment from former relationships and for forming a new alliance. It is a barometer for the marriage as a whole. Someone once suggested that "[m]arriage vows should be changed to say 'as long as we are not bored' instead of 'as long as we both shall live'". That is not God's idea. Oneness is a lifelong process; it does not end when you get tired or bored.

The Bible has a lot to say about marriage. In the opening chapter of Genesis, we see the first marriage, that of Adam and Eve, in the Garden of Eden. "The Lord God said, 'It is not good for the man to be alone. I will make a helper suitable for him.'" (Genesis 2:18) It then goes on to describe how God caused Adam to fall into a deep sleep, took out a rib from him, and formed a companion for him out of it. Eve became the suitable helper, assisting Adam as he took care of the Garden of Eden.

Marriage as Perfect Union

God works through relationships. The first relationship in the Bible is that of the Trinity: God the Father, God the Son, and God the Holy Spirit. The Father loves the Son and gives Him everything. The Son always does that which pleases the Father, including death on the cross. The Holy Spirit takes everything about the Son and reveals it to us. We learn from the Trinity that relationships are the very essence of our existence. We also learn that relationships should be expressed through concern for others. It is God's commitment to relationships that made Him notice Adam's loneliness and provide a partner for Him. God is certainly very interested in the marriage institution because it was His idea in the first place.

Marriage is intended for mutual pleasure, enjoyment, and procreation. God intended for married couples to attain the highest level of satisfaction and fulfilment in their relational needs. Indeed, the marriage relationship is a precious gift from God to which I can testify. Many others can confirm their own joys in the marital union.

Marriage is a publicly acknowledged and socially recognised union between a man and a woman, but it is also more than that. It blends two families, not just two individuals. Although it involves an emotional union, it does not eliminate the individual identities of the partners. How two become one and remain distinct is a mystery that only God can make possible.

God designed marriage to be a reflection of our relationship with Him; He purposed it to be the most peaceful, intimate, and fulfilling relationship in our lives. As beautiful as marriage is, however, it has the capacity to prick—and very painfully. If handled well, though, the joy and fulfilment it brings is worth all the pain.

Roles in Marriage

The Bible defines the roles of both the husband and the wife, clearly spelling out the obligation they have towards each other. In Ephesians, Paul provides married couples with the essential building blocks for establishing a strong marriage. To the wives, he says, "Wives, submit to your husbands as to the Lord. For the husband is the head of the wife as Christ is the head of the church, his body, of which he is the Saviour. Now as the church submits to Christ, so also wives should submit to their husbands in everything." (Ephesians 5:22-24) He also says, "Wives, submit to your husbands, as is fitting in the Lord". (Colossians 3:18)

And to the husbands, he says, "Husbands, love your wives, just as Christ loved the church and gave himself up for her to make her holy, cleansing her by the washing with water through the word, and to present her to himself as a radiant church, without stain or wrinkle or any other blemish, but holy and blameless. In this same way, husbands ought to love their wives as their own bodies. He who loves his wife loves himself." (Ephesians 5:25-28)

Peter provides further counsel by saying, "Wives, in the same way, be submissive to your husbands so that, if any of them do not believe the word, they may be won over without words by the behaviour of their wives, when they see the purity and reverence of your lives. Your beauty should not come from outward adornment, such as braided hair and the wearing of gold jewellery and fine clothes. Instead, it should be that of your inner self, the unfading beauty of a gentle and quiet spirit, which is of great worth in God's sight. For this is the way the holy women of the past who put their hope in God used to make themselves beautiful. They were submissive to their own husbands. ... Husbands, in the same way be considerate as you live with your wives, and treat them with respect as the weaker partner and as heirs with you of the gracious gift of life, so that nothing will hinder your prayers." (1Peter 3:1-5, 7)

Sadly, many women are averse to the concept of submission. When it comes up, it can generate diverse views, opinions, and reactions, including anger and hostility. Although the place of submission in the marriage relationship has been hotly debated, it remains grossly misunderstood. A former classmate of mine observed, "It is time to delete the word 'submission' from the marriage vows because women should not be doormats for their husbands".

It is not hard to see where she comes from. Many husbands believe that certain Bible verses give them leeway to act as they wish and to subject their wives to their whims. Some husbands and wives actually believe that submission indicates that women are inferior to men in some way. I know women who are afraid of submitting to their husbands for fear of losing their identity. Others are afraid that, if they submit to their husbands, they open themselves to abuse.

> *[God] still expects us to honour His commands because, outside of them, we cannot find true fulfilment.*

These notions, however, do not diminish the authority of God's word. He still expects us to honour His commands because, outside them, we cannot find true fulfilment. When God requires the woman to submit to the leadership of the man, He does not suggest that the woman is less important than her husband because she certainly is not. The scriptures (Ephesians 5:22-30 and Colossians 3:18) clarify that a wife is to submit voluntarily to her husband's sensitive and loving leadership. As I voluntarily submit to my husband, I complete him. I help him fulfill his responsibilities; I help him become the man, husband, friend, and leader God intended him to be.

In the name of gender equality, many women have moved away from God's guidelines for living together. Instead, they have opened themselves up to ungodly sources of wisdom. The miserable state of marriages today is a clear testimony of what happens when we depart from godly counsel and wisdom.

Let us briefly look at the roles of the husband and the wife, as they are spelt out in the Bible.

Roles of the Husband

God expects the husband to be a servant leader, protector, and provider. Unfortunately, many husbands offer no leadership to their families. They neglect their responsibilities or their wives do not let them take the leadership. Sometimes, men do not understand their role because their wives have paid jobs and provide for the family as well. These aside, God still expects them to execute their role as He has defined it. When the husband fails to fulfil his role or the wife hinders him from doing so, the marriage suffers.

Paul instructs the husbands to "love your wives, just as Christ loved the church and gave himself up for her" (Ephesians 5:25). He continues to say that they "ought to love their wives as their own bodies. He who loves his wife loves himself." (Ephesians 5:28) In other words, the husband should protect his wife from the outside world—from impurity, physical harm, and anything that might damage their marriage.

The role stipulated above is the ideal role, but there is an assumed role in every home. Not spelling out the assumed role could cause conflict in the home. In the days of my grandparents, roles were clearly articulated: My grandmother tended the farm, fetched water from the river, gathered firewood, and cooked for the family. My grandfather grazed his cattle, often helped at the coffee plantation, and met his male friends at the end of the day.

Today, the man of the house is continually accused of being more and more absent and of abdicating his responsibility as head of the home. When the man is absent and does not take responsibility, the wife has no option but to take up that role herself. In the end, he loses the power to her because she no longer needs him as head of the family. Many wives also seek other men to fill the gaps in their lives, created by their husbands' neglect.

Mercy is a happy girl. What she loves best about her husband is his commitment to providing for and protecting her. She has nothing to worry about because her husband John always sorts out problems that arise. When her car breaks down, she makes a simple phone call and he takes care of it. Her husband is like her life insurance. When she falls sick, he takes her to hospital. He drops the children at school, pays their school fees, and supervises their homework. "What more can I ask for?" Mercy asks. "I feel secure in marriage and advise my friends to marry and enjoy the warmth and fellowship."

When the author of Ecclesiastes asserts that two are better than one and that two keep each other warm (4:11a), I could not agree more. The husband should provide his wife with a safe place to live in, a comfortable and secure home where she can raise a family. In most African societies, if a man has not built his wife a home, then he does not fulfill societal expectations of a true man. Besides providing shelter for his family, God expects a man to supply food, clothing, education, medical care, and other needs for the family.

Roles of the Wife

The wife comes into the marriage team as a helper, a team player, and a nurturer. A helper is perfectly matched to complete a team. Note that both players of the team must be actively involved in the task, making for a lasting marriage. Paul also instructs the wives to "submit to your husbands as to the Lord" (Ephesians 5:22). While many women have a problem with the idea of submission, God still expects it of them and holds them accountable. While submission is expected of wives, it does not mean that husbands are released from loving them according to God's word. They should still look out for their wives' welfare, even if it means giving up their lives for them.

As a wife, you should allow your husband to assume his God-given role, with you coming alongside as his helper. If you decide to lead instead of follow, you go against God's plan for a happy marriage. I did not write the rules. If you disagree, you have to take it up with God, who wrote the rules. Understand that submission does not make you a doormat or a slave. A helper is a player, just like any other player in a team sport. If your husband makes a decision you feel is wrong, you are free to voice your doubt. You, however, have to submit to his decision as long as it is in line with God's word. This is an act of love. God will not only reward you for it, but He will also protect you from harm because of your obedience.

The Bible also places a special emphasis on the need for wives to respect their husbands (Ephesians 5:33). When you respect your husband, you regard him with honour and esteem. This means valuing his opinions, admiring his wisdom and character, appreciating his commitment to his work, friends, and you, and honouring his needs and values. Wives are instructed to love their husbands (Titus 2:4), so when you respect your husband, he will obviously feel loved.

Leave Your Parents and Cleave to Your Partner

For this reason, a man will leave his father and mother and be united to his wife, and they will become one flesh. (Genesis 2:24)

Although scripture talks about the man leaving his parents and is silent on the part of the woman, her own departure from the family home is implied. The need to emphasise more the man's exit may be because he can assume that he does not need to leave his own people, as a family heir. Ruth's words to her mother-in-law Naomi speak clearly for the women: "Where you go I will go, and where you stay I will stay. Your people will be my people and your God my God." (Ruth 1:16)

When a girl gets married in my Kikuyu community, she is given either her childhood bed or a new one, as a gift. It is a reminder to her that she no longer has a bed to come back to in her parents' home; it is a way of saying goodbye. If she visits her family, she would spend the night with them just like any other guest would. The man, on the other hand, does not receive a similar gift to imply his departure because he is actually supposed to bring the bride to his family's homestead.

As I prepared for my own son's wedding, I also readied myself emotionally for his departure. Although he would always be my son, I knew once the day came, he would leave us and cleave to his wife, become one with her, and build their home together. His new core loyalty would be to his wife. That is how my husband and I live. Although his parents may guide us because of their years of experience, they do not make decisions for us.

For a marriage to succeed, both husband and wife must leave the parental home psychologically, emotionally, and physically. They must learn to relate in a new way with their parents and their other parental figures. Because marriage changes their loyalties, the couple must look to each other for support. While love and support from parents, siblings, or close friends remain important, we must recognise that loyalties change. This is what cleaving is all about.

While love and support from parents, siblings, or close friends remain important, we must recognise that loyalties change.

I had the privilege of walking my son down the aisle to marry his beautiful bride. On arrival at the altar, the pastor asked, "Who gives this woman to be married to this man?" My heart leapt within me because the moment symbolised the end of one life stage and the beginning of a new one for him. It was a phase, where I would have little significance but where his wife would take centre stage. Inasmuch as his decision would make or break his dream in life, his loyalties were no longer with us but with his dear wife. I had to undergo a process of coming to terms with the reality and acknowledging the effect of his departure. I let go to make it easier for him to create space for his wife.

Earlier in the day, I had picked up his bride from her home, together with our family and friends. We also picked up a suitcase with her belongings. She was not returning to her father's house; it was goodbye forever. Tears of joy and apprehension were shed, as we sang and danced. Parents and close relatives battled varying emotions. After exchanging pleasantries and gifts, we left with the bride. She is now and forever my son's wife, until death separates them. Years before, I too had left my home and have cleaved to my husband since.

Leaving is not just physical; it is also psychological and emotional. It involves doing away with some patterns of behaviour. While you can maintain your old friendships, you have to set boundaries to them, so you do not create insecurity in the marriage. Complaining about her husband's insecurities, Mary said, "I cannot understand why he complains about my relationship with James. We grew up together; we were best friends. How can he ask me to end the relationship?" Listening to Mary, I understood her husband's apprehension. He is uncomfortable with the relationship simply because the lack of boundaries eats into the marriage.

When Bob and I got married, I easily moved on because my life changed very fast: I became a mother and had a husband, home, extended family, and children to look after. The responsibilities were so enormous, they soon nailed me down. Bob had more freedom, so he continued to live like a single man. His friends played centre stage, which was a source of conflict in the beginning of our relationship. Although I continued to voice my concerns, I was patient. I knew that it was just a matter of time. None of his friends was married then, but once they did, things changed and boundaries shifted automatically.

Leaving comes with challenges. There are positive things from the past to value and negative things to watch out for. The couple must choose what is best for the marriage. The reason for developing the new core loyalty is obvious: Marriage is intended as a beautiful, permanent intimacy that shows the beauty and creativity of God. If we do not disconnect from other relationships that access our hearts, the intimacy between a husband and wife never grows. With all its joys, pains, and difficulties, marriage is a sign that points to our union with God.

As you leave and cleave, look out for the following pitfalls:

1. Relationship with in-laws

Maintain a healthy link with both families. It is important that relationships are developed between them. They must have the opportunity to grow with time and to create good bridges to accommodate each other. I know situations where a husband expects a wife to have nothing to do with her family. This is very dangerous and should not be encouraged.

2. Consultation

It is wrong to do things without consulting your partner. Financial assistance to respective families should be discussed and mutually agreed upon.

3. Extended family

The African home accommodates many extended families. It is wonderful that we are hospitable and that we take care of our siblings. However, it is important that this is discussed and agreed upon by both spouses before any member of the extended family moves in.

4. Decision making

Do not discuss and approve issues with your family before discussing them with your partner. It is important that decisions concerning the family are discussed by the couple.

financial Management in Marriage

Suppose one of you wants to build a tower. Won't you first sit down and estimate the cost to see if you have enough money to complete it?
Luke 14:28

Money is part of our lives. No matter what we do, we cannot escape the subject. Even Solomon observes, "... Money is the answer for everything". (Ecclesiastes 10:19b) With this in mind, it is important to recognise that it needs to be handled with prudence and integrity. If it is not managed well, it becomes a source of conflict in relationships, particularly in marriage. Finance is a very important element of any successful marriage, so it is advisable to share your plans with your spouse for a happy and financially secure marriage.

Merging of finances

Financial management in marriage is a very complex subject, complicated by the fact that two people enter into marriage with different financial needs, values, and expectations. Once the two become one flesh, it becomes necessary to become one in finances, too. This is usually easier for a younger couple with few assets, but for the couple that had worked for a long time, acquired possessions, and established sound individual finances, things can be more complicated because they have their own goals for financial fulfilment. The latter already have a pattern of financial management; they are used to spending money without consulting anyone.

Marriage provides the opportunity for two people to merge their respective incomes and have a joint vision of anticipated earnings and expenditure, including a financial plan for the new family. You and your husband should discuss obligations, net worth, dreams, short- and long-term goals, expectations, current incomes, and other compensations at the beginning of your life together. This eliminates potential problems and meets your future objectives.

Expenditure generally focuses on rent, mortgage, household goods, utilities, groceries, entertainment, and gifts. Sometimes, it also includes support of extended family and future financial goals. More often than not, partners do not disclose their income and expenditure to one another. From my experience, couples that disclose their financial income and expenditure have less trouble than those that do not because their honesty provides an opportunity to plan accurately.

Financial Decisions

Money is hardly ever enough. It requires combined effort to have stress-free financial planning. Money decisions can build relationships as easily as they can break them. A relationship built over many years can be destroyed easily by one financial disagreement. Equally, a lifelong relationship can emerge from a financial favour offered and received at a time of need.

Marriage is not exempt from money's ability to build or destroy relationships. In marriage, money decisions affect each partner's outlook. It can lead to separation or divorce just as easily as it can offer an opportunity for spouses to draw closer to each other. Since money can be a major cause of marital friction, it is important for a couple to learn how to handle money together.

People relate to money differently. Largely, our spending is greatly influenced by our upbringing, culture, and environment. Our attitude towards money is greatly affected by the way we saw and heard our parents handle money. Indeed, most people use their parents' model of handling finances.

> *In marriage, money decisions ... can lead to separation or divorce just as easily as it can draw [spouses] closer to each other.*

Our different backgrounds, beliefs, and value systems also determine our financial management skills. With this in mind, it is not hard to see why two people from varying backgrounds are likely to disagree on money matters. Money issues are some of the biggest challenges faced by marriages today.

While my own personal experience concerning finances in marriage may not represent that of most wives, I choose to share it here because it has worked for me.

When I got married, my husband and I never discussed finances. As soon as I received my salary at the end of each month, I dutifully handed it over to him to allocate it as he saw fit. Nobody taught me what I needed to do with my money in marriage, so I continued to do what I had always done with my money, only replacing my father with my husband. When I lived with my father, he handled my money for me. When I got my first cheque, he opened a bank account on my behalf. He was a banker, so I believed that he knew how to handle money. He gave me what I needed for my daily expenses and banked the rest for me.

When I got married, the only thing that changed was my money manager; otherwise, I continued with the same practice. Without being asked, I gave Bob my entire salary. I never even opened the envelope in which it came. My experience with my father led me to believe that the man of the house dealt with the finances. By God's mercy, this system worked for us. Nothing was mine or his; everything was always ours!

I do not suggest that this is the way to handle family finances. I was young and my needs were basic. With time, however, the situation changed. As I grew older, my needs also grew; I needed my money, which I could use freely without being very accountable. Other needs for investments also came up. As Bob and I grew both in marriage and in our finances, so did our financial needs and management change. This continues to evolve. What is important is to agree on how things ought to be administered. Participation in decision making is key to averting any conflicts.

Shared Testimonies

Couples have different ways of handling money. Whatever method they adopt comes with its own challenges, if basic principles of money management are not observed. Here are some experiences I have recorded from my marriage fitness seminars.

"Our biggest arguments are always about money," Clara told me. "My husband accuses me of being a poor money manager. I have to explain and justify every little purchase I make: groceries, our children's toys, or personal items. In an effort to get out of the financial bondage, I started a business. The venture failed. Since I had borrowed a lot of money to start it, I ran into deep debt, which I kept a secret from my husband for a long time, before I finally confessed to him. Although he understood and forgave me in the end, he flings it back to my face, whenever we disagree on anything, especially financial. Oh, how it hurts!"

Joan, who went the way of the joint account, said, "When we operated a joint bank account, my husband would withdraw money without my knowledge and spend it as he wished. This caused so much conflict that I decided to have my own separate account. When I did that, he stopped contributing to the family finances. I now have to pay the rent, buy groceries, maintain my car, and do about everything else by myself. I cannot remember when he last gave me any money. I now wonder why I have him in the house at all; he is a liability."

Mary, a diligent high school teacher and her husband John, who was also a teacher, met at an early age, married, and were blessed with three children. Their greatest ambition in life was to own their own home. They decided to save some money on a monthly basis towards their goal, but John somehow always found a reason to withdraw money from the account. He never bothered to explain to his wife what he needed it for. In the meantime, their children were growing up and Mary's desire to have her own home intensified. Their savings venture having failed, she decided to borrow money from a cooperative savings society and use it to construct a simple, three-bedroom house. The loan was approved. As soon as the money was credited into her account, she shared the good news with her husband. He too was delighted.

Plans to build the house were discussed and an architect was hired to design the house. In a little while, the builders would be on site. As this went on, John was hardly at home and often spent nights away from the family. With financing from his wife's loan, he had found himself a girlfriend in the same neighbourhood, which was an embarrassment to the family. The construction money vanished and the project never took off.

As these three women found out, love and trust are two very different things. Another lady shared, "There are no guarantees in marriage anymore. You may be married to a particular person, but he is only yours during moments when he is present. When he is not with you, he could be playing husband to someone else."

While many couples manage their finances prudently, lack of trust between couples is an everyday reality in many marriages. With so many documented cases of financial abuse, it is understandable that many wives do not trust their husbands concerning financial matters. Njoki shared, "I learnt that it is best for a married couple to own things separately. My father was very abusive towards my mum. She slept many nights in the cold, following beatings she constantly received. My father never spared her even in our presence. Despite our relatives' and friends' interventions, nothing worked. One day, in the course of another beating, my mother fell down the staircase and broke her leg and collarbone. By the time she recovered, she had made up her mind: Enough was enough.

"One morning, after my father had left for up-country on his regular business trips, my mother called his siblings and asked them to collect their brother's belongings. No persuasion from the family could make her change her mind; she was not living with him another day. His stuff eventually ended up in a godown in the industrial area. My mother posted a guard at the gate to ensure that he did not get into the compound at any time. My father never returned to our home. He could do nothing. I learnt later that my mother owned our house; she had taken a loan long ago and paid for it in full. I hate to imagine what would have happened to her had the house been in my dad's name."

From her mother's experience, Njoki has become a great believer in couples owning property individually. She owns a flat, whose mortgage she services. She would never consider joint ownership of marital property. From my mother's example, my own preference is to possess things jointly. I believe each couple should find what works for them as long as it safeguards the family's future, especially the children's. It may be helpful to understand the legal implications of owning property individually or jointly before engaging in a purchase. Your lawyer should give you the pros and cons.

The place to discuss matters of finance and investment is at the very beginning of a marriage. Review them periodically to decide which option works best for both of you. Whatever decision you make, remember that God intended marriage to be a permanent relationship. It should not be viewed in any way as a temporary relationship, which can end because of difficulties or boredom. Remember that you vowed to stay in marriage, for richer or poorer.

Relationship and Financial Reflection

How is your relationship with your partner as far as finances are concerned? Do you or do you not openly discuss money issues together? Do you make financial decisions together concerning small and big investments? Does one person generally decide on finances in the home? Do you operate a joint account?

Your answers to these questions can help you see where you stand with your partner on money matters. If you find some unease and tension whenever you try to broach matters of family finances, it would be best to try and work it out immediately. Open communication concerning financial commitments can help avert money-related conflicts. It is common today for partners to commit themselves financially without the knowledge or consent of the other. In some instances, these secret commitments end up with auctioneers showing up at the door, when it is already too late to deal with the loss of family assets. This, of course, leads to much heartache and many breakups. Survivors limp along in an atmosphere of emotional and physical disconnection, where the only things remaining are the children and the roof over their heads.

Guidelines on Financial Management in Marriage

1. Discuss/evaluate financial matters before marriage

From the onset of your marriage, know the financial status of your partner: his income, assets, liabilities (particularly details of outstanding debts), and major expenses. It is important to discuss your money-handling habits. This reveals the spending habits of your partner, too. Do you shop impulsively or strategically? It is helpful to talk about experiences with money: how you grew up and what spending or saving meant to you. Be as candid and as open as you possibly can.

2. Plan and take responsibility for your finances

A good and sound financial plan is the only way to maintain financial health. Planning should be done at the very beginning of the marital journey. The Bible counsels, "Suppose one of you wants to build a tower. Won't you first sit down and estimate the cost to see if you have enough money to complete it?" (Luke 14:28)

Many financial burdens and stresses can be traced back to lack of or poor financial planning. Far too often, we live for today and forget about tomorrow. Every couple should set and pursue financial goals that meet their needs. Without financial goals and specific plans on achieving them, we leave our future to chance. According to Proverbs 14:15, "... the prudent give thought to their steps". It is important to make short-term, medium, and long-term financial goals together. Frequent reviews of financial plans and goals are important because you cannot track progress without them.

3. Assess your financial needs together

At the beginning of your relationship, set realistic financial and investment goals together. I encourage all couples not only to discuss about their finances but also to write them down. They should have sound financial plans and anticipated outcomes. Unfortunately, it is not the norm for couples to talk about finances; it is often left to the man of the house to handle them, a result of value systems handed down from fathers, grandfathers, and great grandfathers. My grandfather told me, "Maitu, kuri maundu mamwe materaguo atumia". (Mum, there are certain things that women are not told!) Some of these things pertain to finances.

4. Consult and set financial boundaries

Financial boundaries are as important as other boundaries in your marital relationship. It is important for the couple to define what constitutes a major purchase. Joyce decided she had had it with her ill-maintained car. Impulsively, she decided to leave the car at a garage, went to a car dealer, and came out with a new vehicle! When her husband came home to find a new car purchased without his consent, he sent Joyce packing after a big fight that left her permanently scarred.

For some people, spending their last paycheck without planning for or discussing it is inconsequential but, for others, it is a major decision. Whichever way you look at it, such impulsive spending can lead to serious consequences. I have seen many people charge large amounts of money on their credit cards without discussing the expenditure with their partners. Do you consider it appropriate to consult your partner, when making a purchase, donating money, or simply giving away gifts? The bottom line is that you should set your financial boundaries as a couple from day one and continue to evaluate them as you grow through life. When people know how far they can go without consulting their partner, it reduces financial challenges.

finances and Significant Others or the Extended family

In our cultural setting, significant others are part of our families. They include parents, siblings, uncles, and aunties on both sides of the marriage. Financial assistance to them is often necessary but, although it is a good thing, it also serves as a major financial challenge in many marriages, which cannot be ignored. It is important to engage in this subject and set parameters for your participation. This can be reviewed on an ongoing basis, but the basic principle is to remain open about any financial involvement. It can destroy the relationship when a partner discovers that his money has been channelled without his knowledge to assist the extended family.

Maggie and David have been married for several years. Like most families, they struggled to pay their mortgage and educate their children. They hardly had any money left for their savings. What Maggie never told David is that she had taken on the burden to educate her younger siblings, since her parents were not economically empowered. For Maggie, it was something that she did when she was single; she did not see the need to discuss it with her husband. According to her, he came from an able family and would not see the sense of taking on the burden when they struggled with their own children's fees. When her husband eventually found out about the arrangement, he was thoroughly upset. He had never had reason to doubt her financial fidelity. He often wondered, "What else has she been keeping secret from me?"

For many, it is common to have the husband's relatives living with the family. Joyce returned home one day to find that her husband's two brothers had moved in with them, without any warning from her husband. They were weekend guests, who eventually stayed on for three years. It turned out that their brother had actually invited them to come and stay. The couple's privacy was invaded. The brothers' upkeep depleted their finances and the couple's relationship deteriorated. It is, therefore, important that the couple consult one another on any matter that has a financial implication. In the absence of consultation, it opens opportunities for serious conflicts.

Budgeting

A budget tells you how much the anticipated or actual income is and gives a detailed proposal of the expenditure. It is helpful to record all household expenses, such as utilities, clothing, gifts, donations, fees, medical insurance, and any other recurring expenses. Budgeting ensures financial discipline.

Early in our marriage, Bob and I neither operated on a budget nor kept records of income and expenditure. Then one day, our finances became a glaring concern. To rein in things, we decided to record every income and expenditure no matter how small. Over a period of three months, we discovered shocking things: We spent much more than our income on things we did not really need. Our greatest expenditure were gifts and contributions towards social events and fundraisers. The figures were unbelievable! We went back to the drawing board, made an evaluation, and started all over again. We decided to reevaluate our giving habits carefully and to support needy cases within our budget. It took a long time to become financially secure again, but we came out wiser. We tightened our belts and cut down where we needed to do so. Eventually, our efforts paid off and we got our breakthrough.

I encourage you to keep good financial records. You can use computer software to help you analyse your financial status. There are many of them readily available in the market.

Before embarking on budget planning, it is advisable to track your expenses. That way, the budget items are realistic and are based on actual situations. Many times, the reason we fail to follow our budget is because it does not represent the reality. Tracking expenses also helps in easily identifying obvious spending areas that can be reduced or eliminated.

The expense tracker is used to key in monthly expenses. It assists you in determining how much you actually spend. The simplest way to do it would be to write down daily expenses. Carry a notebook with you and document what you spend on every day, including newspapers and coffees. This exercise also helps you categorise your expenses.

For expenses, such as insurance, which are not paid on a frequent basis, divide the price into monthly contributions. Once you have come up with your own expense tracker, compare this with your ideal budget and make the necessary adjustments to align both the expenses and the budget. What is important is to ensure that you do not spend more than you earn. If the income does not meet your budgetary projections, discuss the matter with your spouse and strike out nonessentials. In such a case, it is of utmost importance to agree on what constitutes a nonessential.

Sample Budget Guidelines and Expense Tracker

Spending **60%** *(expenses)*

Investing **40%** (tithes, savings, investments, and giving)

Hypothetical Salary **KES 50,000/month**

EXPENSE ITEM	%	ALLOTTED AMOUNT
Tithes	10	5,000
Housing	15	7,500
Insurance	5	2,500
Transportation	2	1,000
Debt servicing	5	2,500
Groceries	8	4,000
Medical	3	1,500
Entertainment	10	5,000
School/children	5	2,500
Grooming	4	2,000
Gifts	3	1,500
Savings	10	5,000
Investments	15	7,500
Giving, parents	2.5	1,250
Giving, poor	2.5	1,250
Total	**100**	**50,000**

N.B. KES 85 = USD 1

Who Is in Charge of the Budget?

As part of planning, it is important to decide who maintains the budget, handles the bills, and keeps records. I have always been keen on our family's financial records and my husband has always trusted me to handle that. I am aware that, generally, men like to keep the chequebook and handle the money issues, which is fine. It is customary in many African traditions, so a change in the system may go against cultural values and beliefs. I have also interacted with many men who recognise that their wives are better at keeping financial controls and records than they are, so they have given them the financial responsibility. It is important to acknowledge and appreciate gifting and apportion duty accordingly, regardless of gender. Determine what works for you and go with it.

Understand Financial Planning

Financial planning involves spending and saving future income. This plan allocates future income to various types of expenses, such as mortgage, rent, or utilities. It also reserves some income for short- and long-term savings or investments. Many people are ignorant about handling finances. Just as a house needs a strong foundation to withstand the elements, so do you need a solid financial foundation to survive crises. A financial foundation requires that you cover the basics. Remember that financial planning is a continuous process of wisely managing your finances to achieve your life goals and aspirations. It is a journey, which shifts at various stages of your life. It is fun and fulfilling to look back and see your financial achievements individually and as a couple, so let me encourage you to plan.

Know how to stretch your money by getting maximum value from it at all times. Planning requires that you be informed. Do your best to understand the dynamics of borrowing and lending in the money market. Planning helps the couple to have foreknowledge of anticipated income and expenditure, so they can make informed financial decisions. Many get into debt without understanding the consequences of getting a bank loan and not repaying! A debt is not something that you can wish away and, no matter how long you run, the financier will catch up with you.

Create a Contingency Plan

Most people do not have the discipline of saving or a savings plan because they spend everything they earn. Saving is an important discipline in life and the essence of responsibility. Life is full of surprises. With this in mind, always plan to be financially prepared for any eventuality.

It is advisable to have a minimum of six months' salary in a savings account in case you lose your job, the car needs a major repair, or a medical emergency creeps up on you. It is also sensible to save between 10 and 20 percent of your total income on a monthly basis. If, for any reason, you cannot save in a particular month, you should tighten your belt in the following months to cover the missed month.

One way to cut expenses in order to save is to list all your expenses in a month. The list should include items such as transport, food, entertainment, gifts, and donations, for a period of at least three months. In doing so, you can scrutinise the expenditure and decide where to cut down. I know parents who pool cars to transport their children to school or to attend other functions. This reduces the expenses on transport, and you can save money.

The Discipline of Saving

The discipline of saving is important and should be diligently exercised. It is about consistently setting aside money for future use. Saving money is the foundation for financial success. It determines your economic status of either living in abundance or in want. For most people, saving money is not easy. It comes with discipline and consistency, especially with ever-increasing financial obligations and the inflation around us. Saving money over a lifetime requires conscious effort and continued awareness so that it becomes a habit. Exercising this as individuals and as a couple should be taken very seriously.

The cost of borrowing money from the banks today continues to rise. You can obtain a loan or mortgage at anywhere between 14 to 17 percent interest. At the end of five to 10 years, you would have paid a very high interest on it. Although we cannot do without borrowing, it is helpful to raise some capital for the investment.

See this scenario:

Suppose you want to borrow KES 1,000,000.00, at an interest rate of 15 percent, payable in 20 years. If you make equal monthly payments and do not make any extra payments within the repayment period, you would have paid a total of KES 3,160,295.00. Out of that, the total interest paid would be KES 2,160,295.00. The cost of borrowing would be drastically reduced, if you had a significant amount of savings.

Plan for the Savings Together

Once you build your savings, you need to plan for it. The savings can be banked in a savings account or a fixed deposit account. It can also be put into assets, such as treasury bills, bonds, stocks, and shares. Plan as a couple on how to spend it, if you had not already done so. The savings can be used to help the couple go on a holiday, buy a new car, buy land, or finish a home project.

By taking time to discuss simple steps at the beginning of your life together, you can eliminate potential problems and meet your long-term goals. Share your plans for a happy and financially secure marriage.

Invest for the Future

When you are able to save money, it is advisable to invest some of it for the future. One of the books that inspires me is *The Millionaire Next Door* by Thomas Stanley and William Danko. They share about common denominators among those who successfully build wealth. The denominators are that (1) They live below their means, and (2) They believe that financial independence is more important than displaying social status. The greatest challenge today is keeping up with the Joneses. Most people live beyond their means, displaying social status and struggling to stay afloat.

The investment you make now determines the quality of your future. Remember always that a time will come when you will not have the energy that you have today, so live within your means, and enjoy stability and a comfortable future.

Earthly Things

In writing this chapter, I visited some of my good friends who had lost their beloved father. I could not help but think of how temporary our lives are on earth. The title of a song by Jim Reeves, *This World Is Not My Home*, rang so true. No wonder Job said, "Naked I came from my mother's womb, and naked I will depart" (Job 1:21). Hold lightly to earthly things!

God is the giver of every good and perfect gift, so we give Him all the glory and honour for allowing us to be custodians of His precious gifts in this world. We must never lose sight of that and turn to worship our earthly wealth. Once we recognise that everything belongs to God and that He can take them away, we will find it easier to share what we have with other people, starting with our spouses.

Writing a Will

As I write this chapter, I have just lost a colleague. We said our goodbyes for the weekend with a cheerful "See you on Monday". The Monday meeting never materialised; he died in a road accident over the weekend. I cannot help but think about his young wife and her devastating sense of loss. For all the pain it brings, death remains a present reality in our lives. Just as surely as tomorrow comes, so will death come for each of us—ready or not. Our days are numbered; we have no way of knowing what tomorrow holds for us.

Issues of inheritance can be a thorn in the flesh. Unless they are clearly articulated by the deceased, they can be a cause of much misery to the family. Many wives have been left almost destitute after the passing on of their husbands. Apparently, it is still not customary for Africans to write wills. Understand that your legacy plans as a single person are unlikely to work after marriage, so prepare for death's eventuality. Consider writing a will. Talk about it with your spouse and seek the advice of your lawyer. Decisions of inheritance should be openly discussed.

Raising Up Children

Children are a heritage from the LORD,
offspring a reward from him.
Like arrows in the hands of a warrior
are children born in one's youth.
Psalm 127:3-4

G od's gift of marriage is not only for pleasure but also for procreation. God expects us to "increase and multiply". Bringing forth and raising children are satisfying tasks in life. It has been a great joy and privilege for me and my husband to bring up three children of our own and others of close relatives. Children are a gift from God; no couple has a guarantee that they will have children. It is for this reason that the gift of children ought to be appreciated and the children raised up well.

Parenthood is itself a special gift. God intended that the human race be preserved through marriage between one man and one woman. He expects the union to bring forth godly offspring. We should all be concerned by contemporary trends that abuse the institution of marriage. First is the push towards gay and lesbian marriages. Even sadder is the fact that some women are not keen on motherhood for fear of losing their figures and body image. Many are terrified by the inevitable sagging of the bosom from breastfeeding and the threat to career opportunities. I know a couple who have only one child. The husband wants more children, but the wife will hear none of it. She reasons, "I am taking care of my body!"

With all due respect to women who feel this way, I still believe that being a mother goes beyond anything imaginable. It is a special, God-given gift—a miracle that surpasses human understanding. To hold your child in your hands is such a beautiful feeling; it strengthens the marriage bond because it is the fruit of love and marriage.

It is not automatic that, when you get married, you will have children. There are many women like Hannah (1 Samuel 1:10-11), who cry out to the Lord to bless them with a child. If the Lord has blessed you with the ability to have children, enjoy motherhood. You never know what you can bring forth. Your child could be a latter-day Moses or the president of a nation in their generation! The psalmist says, "Their children will be mighty in the land; the generation of the upright will be blessed" (Psalm 112:2).

My greatest joy and fulfillment in life is having mothered children myself—wonderful, sensitive, caring, and accomplished children. I was even blessed with twins! Other than my own, I have two adorable grandchildren. Bob and I considered our duty of parenting to be of utmost importance. The privilege of raising and mentoring the children was our priority and, for us, the definition of success was in bringing up children who would become responsible and well-rounded citizens.

It is amazing just how fast time passes. It seems only yesterday when we were busy with the children, struggling to ensure that they get a good education and training them to become responsible and excellent children in all aspects of life. Now they are all young adults who have left home and have already started their own families.

I still recall the day I came home to the aroma of delicious food filling the air. As I walked in, I noticed that the dining table was set only for two. Then the absence of my children hit me. Traditionally, my family dined together on Mondays. This particular Monday was especially significant because Bob and I were in a thanksgiving mood over a recent success. That night, though, we were the only guests at the dinner table. As we dined together, we reflected on the journey of parenthood and acknowledged that, although parenting is a lifelong journey, our direct parenting roles had already ended. Our children were now adults in their own homes. We were thankful that our children did not just grow up; they actually turned out right. We are often asked, "How did you do it?" It was trial and error for us and a lot of God's favour!

A card hangs from the wall of our house—a card I have kept over the years. I treasure it greatly because it was given to us by our children. It reads:

> *To Mom and Dad:*
> *Thank you for being such wonderful parents*
> *Nothing we say or do can measure our gratitude*
> *Not silver or gold can repay*
> *Thanks for being there for us,*
> *We shall forever be thankful ... grateful to both of you*
> *One of the things that made you such great parents*

Is that you were partners in everything
In life, in love, in small and big things
In raising us as a family
You shared responsibilities,
The decisions and, most of all, the joys
And in doing so, you made our family strong
Your love held us all together, made us feel secure
Supported us and encouraged
us to pursue our dreams
We are grateful to
both of you for being
Such caring, thoughtful, and committed individuals
And sharing, loving parents
Monday dinners we shall miss
but, in our hearts,
we are joined in
love and unity forever
We shall always look forward!

What a treasure children are! We do not go to school to learn how to bring up children. All parents use their own social experiences, leaving out what they did not like and applying what appealed to them. Every parent wants the best for their children, but the result makes the statement. Did you make a positive impact? It is not easy being a parent, especially if one seeks perfection. We continue learning along the way of parenting.

Raising my children was no ordinary responsibility. I was young, pursuing an education. I had a business to run, a husband to take care of, and a full-time job. Like many working mothers, I faced the challenge of spending many hours away from home. My children spent time with the house help, whom I appreciated greatly. I made up the time with the children every evening and during the weekends, as I found appropriate. The quality time we spent together was a time of teaching, correcting, and instructing.

Parenting Responsibility

Parenting is not the sole responsibility of the mother; it is the responsibility of both parents. Every parent plays a significant role in the emotional growth of children, so they must play their individual roles. The father, who is the head of the family, ought to take responsibility in this area. He should interact with the children as much as possible and be present. It is from this interaction that a close bond between the father and the children develops. The bond has a great impact on how the children end up becoming in later years. Many parents seek close union with their children a little too late, not having played their roles in the early years. As a result, they face the children's rejection and disobedience.

Raising children can be fun, especially before they begin to grapple with homework and peer pressure. Playing with children below the age of seven helps them grow into creative and unique individuals. They also grow in confidence, learn to communicate well, and develop positive attitudes towards life. Happy children reduce the stress of parents and allow them to relax and enjoy parenting.

Children are particularly sensitive to their parents' moods. They can sense their joy and their anger. They may not speak out, but they can feel the vibes, when there is a disagreement in the home. They are very sensitive, too, and well aware of their mother's mood, not only after they are born but even while still in the womb! They know their mother's temperaments, which also affect their own moods.

My grandmother once described to me how her husband, my grandfather, had taken care of her when she was pregnant. Apparently, Kikuyu culture dictates that a man be at his wife's side until the baby is born. Although my grandfather had his own hut, he would spend the nights at her house, whenever she expected a baby. It was an opportunity to be pampered, caressed, and nurtured. According to grandma, the pregnancy periods were great because her husband really indulged her.

Parents are the most influential role models in their children's lifetime, so they must demonstrate kindness, respect, honesty, hospitality, and generosity to them. What we teach our children goes many generations down the line because they will teach the same to their children and their children's children. Children become what you bring them up to become. When you do not teach them proper habits when they are little, you cannot expect them to become respectable citizens in the future. As I grew up, my parents instilled in us as children the values of hard work, integrity, and honesty.

Developing the Right Values in Children

As the Bible teaches, if we bring up our children in the ways of the Lord, then they will not depart from them even when they grow old (Proverbs 22:6). Another proverb admonishes children: "Listen, my son, to your father's instruction and do not forsake your mother's teaching." (Proverbs 1:8) A solid foundation is, therefore, very important where the children's discipline is concerned.

Discipline is important when bringing up children. Through it, they learn to distinguish between acceptable and unacceptable behaviour. Uncorrected bad behaviour becomes a habit that cannot be changed in the future. For instance, if a child has a habit of destroying things unnecessarily, you must stop them from doing so as soon as possible. It is important to set boundaries for them, so they may know how to behave, whether or not you are around them. Discipline demands consistency and hard work from both sides. It is the only way that you can produce a child who is well-ordered and not a disappointment to you.

My mother once told me the story of a young man. He was so indisciplined, he went to jail in his teen years for stealing. As he stood in the dock, listening to the judge's sentence, he requested permission to say something to his mother. The judge obliged. He leaned over as if to whisper something to her, but to everyone's surprise, he bit off her ear instead. Asked why he had done such a thing, he responded, "My mother never taught me that stealing is bad. If she had, I would not go to jail today." The moral of the story was that my mother had a responsibility to ensure that I conformed—although I disliked discipline—lest I bite off her ear one day!

Finding time to spend together with your children can be

[I]f we bring up our children in the ways of the Lord, then they will not depart from them even when they grow old.

difficult. In the rat race of society today, there is so much to do and so little time. Unfortunately, when time passes, it cannot come back. Time is very expensive because it can never be retrieved. It helps to schedule time for your children. Take your children to school, so you can share that time to talk to one another. While school transport providers are helpful and reduce your time constraints, do schedule to take your children to school sometimes. You can take turns with your husband: One drops them off and the other picks them up. Alternatively, you can work out a weekly or monthly duty rota.

Until our children finished their secondary education, Bob always dropped them off at school and I picked them up. When we look back today, we acknowledge that that was probably the best investment we made as far as our relationship with our children is concerned. We no longer pick them up from school, but we treasure the moments we shared during those years. Their ride to and from school was a great opportunity to catch up, to know how their day went and how they were. The children also treasured the time. It was so special to them that they were against us giving anyone a lift or carpooling because they just wanted to be alone with us. It was their time, a great opportunity to share their challenges and achievements. That moment provided great bonding and fellowship opportunities for our family.

Teaching Obedience to Children

Children, obey your parents in everything, for this pleases the Lord. (Colossians 3:20)

One reason God blessed Abraham was because he would be the father of a godly generation. Raising obedient children requires us to command them to do right, not merely to suggest to them and let them choose what they think is best. God Himself spells out the importance of right parenting for the achievement of His covenant purpose: "For I have chosen him, so that he will direct his children and his household after him to keep the way of the Lord by doing what is right and just, so that the Lord will bring about for Abraham what He has promised him." (Genesis 18:19)

1Timothy 3:2-7 spells out the necessary qualifications for someone involved in a ministry or church administration. One of them has to do with the behaviour of his children. He must "be above reproach, the husband of but one wife, temperate, self-controlled, respectable, hospitable, able to teach, not given to drunkenness, not violent but gentle, not quarrelsome, not a lover of money. He must manage his own family well and see that his children obey him with proper respect." (3:2-4) It is your responsibility as a parent to train your children to obey your word and show you respect. If you do not, you will be to blame for destroying your child. "Discipline your son, for in that there is hope; do not be a willing party to his death." (Proverbs 19:18)

Use the Rod

"Spare the rod and spoil the child" is a well-known saying that highlights discipline as a major aspect in guaranteeing your child's success in life. Paul Hauck, in *How to Bring Up Your Child Successfully*, says, "An undisciplined life is a wasted life and it is bound to be an unproductive life". You certainly want to bring up a child who is productive and who lives a fruitful life—an achiever. When children fail to obey, they must be corrected. It is part of the training process, so they learn to do right. The Bible highly recommends the use of a rod of correction (Proverbs 13:24) as a means of dealing with defiance. We call it spanking. Contemporary ideas on parenting may change every few years, but the Bible never changes. The rod of correction, properly and prayerfully used by a loving parent, produces emotionally healthy and happy children.

In life, there are consequences to wrongdoing, all of which bring much pain. Children need to learn early, which is why we should spank them. If you still feel that children should not be spanked, here is what the word of God says, "Folly is bound up in the heart of a child, but the rod of discipline will drive it far from him" (Proverbs 22:15). Scripture also says, "Do not withhold discipline from a child; if you punish them with the rod, they will not die. Punish them with the rod and save them from death." (Proverbs 23:13-14) There is more: "A rod and a reprimand impart wisdom, but a child left undisciplined disgraces its mother." (Proverbs 29:15) I pray that you allow these verses to be the basis of your decision, regarding your children's discipline.

These are some spanking guidelines:

- Spanking children is not punishment for their wrong but a way to correct them. Never spank a child for an innocent mistake or an accident. Spank only in response to a rebellious, disobedient act to a clearly defined and known rule. You should have clear rules for your children.

- Parents should say what they mean and mean what they say, without raising their voice or constantly threatening their children. If children do not respect their parents' word, it will be difficult for them to respect God's word.

- Never spank your children, unless they know beforehand what is expected of them. Make sure they realise what they did wrong. They must understand that the spanking is a consequence of their choice to disobey a clear, known rule, not the result of their parents' anger.

- Never spank children when you are angry and not in complete control of your emotions.

- After a spanking, always hug your children. Tell them you love them and pray with them. Train them to ask God to forgive them for their wrongs. Children can sometimes throw tantrums that cause you to react harshly towards them. Be gentle and, if necessary, walk away from them when they overreact, instead of being upset and dealing with them right at that moment.

Schedules and Routine

Keep a regular schedule of meals, naps, and bedtimes. If you have to change the schedules, warn the children about it ahead of time. Children tend to work better when they know their schedules. Times for homework should be strictly guided and followed. This is one area where the father plays a very important role. You ought to encourage him to participate. He should use this opportunity to guide and mentor the children as they do their homework. This helps develop the children's character and personality. They become confident because of the father's participation.

As I write this book, I am parenting a preteen boy. He always wants to know what he needs to do and what he must do once he is done. It was the same with my own children. Children thrive on schedules. Schedules build stability and confidence in them, as it lets them know what to expect next. They instil discipline in a nonthreatening manner.

Good schedules should accommodate playtime, study time, and any other activity that you want for them. Consider having dinner together as a family at least once a week, where all of you can catch up and enjoy each other's company. Regular dinner together is, of course, the best option. During this time, it is a good idea for everyone to talk together, regardless of age.

Quality time is very important. Children like to have special days planned for special activities. Keep up with their needs and find a way of facilitating their fun time by being able to swing, swim, or ride with them. Or you can simply watch them as they bounce on a castle.

Showing Affection

When I was growing up, open displays of emotion were not the norm. I was often not appreciated and the focus was always on my wrongs. Breaking a plate caused me so much trouble that I often wondered what the big deal was. A hug never came my way, even when I went to boarding school and my parents visited me there. Hugging is very important and is something that I greatly advocate.

At every given opportunity ... appreciate your children and let them know that you love them...

When parents express emotions and affection, their children learn that it is okay to do the same. Affection is something that flows freely in our home and this helps in affirming the children and making them feel loved and secure in the relationship. When the children feel secure, then the result is a good, trusting bond with the parents. At every given opportunity, therefore, appreciate your children and let them know that you love them and that they mean a great deal to you. Do this to them, regardless of their age. Communicating love is a very powerful parenting agent; it builds up the children's self-esteem. Individuals grow in self-confidence if they feel valued and appreciated.

Listening to the Children

If you listen to your children, you communicate to them that you are interested in what they have to say. More importantly, you make them feel important to you. Whatever you do, do not dismiss them or their opinions. They are intelligent and very sensitive and they usually know what they want. Respect their views. If you do not agree with what they say, explain the reasons for your disagreement and reason with them.

Aside from teaching children about life, we must also know how to respond to their questions. When children ask questions, listen to them carefully and encourage them. Do not shut them off; they learn by observing and by asking questions, and your helpful response to them makes a big difference. Do not dismiss them or be too busy to listen. They may express frustration and stop sharing their thoughts and feelings with you, which may become a major obstacle between you and your children. More often than not, they block you out and open communication becomes nonexistent. In that event, you lose the opportunity as a parent to know your children or even to understand them. This trend may continue into their adolescence and adulthood.

Guidelines on Raising Healthy and Happy Children

How do you actually raise children? In my experience, there is no one right way to do it. And there is no such thing as perfect parents or perfect children, but I have found the following guidelines helpful in raising healthy and happy children.

1. Make your children feel safe

Comfort the children when they are scared. Show them you have taken steps to protect them. Children tend to pick up even the slightest noise. They are sensitive to quiet conversations between you and your husband. When you think they are not listening, they may have an ear to the keyhole. As much as possible, avoid quarrelling or shouting at each other at all times. Do not use the children to fight your battles. Children pick up the vibes very early in their lives.

2. Praise your children

When your children learn something new or behave well, tell them you are proud of them; affirm and reward them. My children never enjoyed sports or other activities, when I was not around to watch them. They wanted my attention, my affirmation, and my participation. I am a guardian of my 10-year-old nephew whom I recently took for a swim. Swimming together with him made him so happy that he continued to thank me long afterwards. He now looks forward to beating me in a swim. Because I took personal interest and continually encouraged him, he has now become a great swimmer; he has won several medals.

When your children do something wrong, criticise the behaviour, not the children themselves. When your child makes a mistake, do not say, "You were bad". Instead, explain what they did wrong. For example, when they choose watching TV over doing homework, explain the house rules and the consequences of not adhering to them. That gets the desired result better than shouting and telling them how awful they are.

3. Be consistent at all times

Come up with house rules that are realistic and which work for your family. Be original and creative. Believe in what you adopt. Whatever they are, be sure that the children understand your expectations clearly. Equally important, be consistent in applying your rules. Consistency also dictates that both parents apply the same rules. If you have other people in the house who supervise the children—house assistants, family members, or relatives—ensure that they know and observe your family rules. Never change the rules midstream, as it can confuse your children. If a rule must be changed, though, it is okay. Just explain such changes to the child beforehand.

Nothing destroys the children's confidence towards their parents more than when the parents do not keep their promises. Children take promises very seriously. When you promise to give them something, especially in appreciation for something well done, never take it lightly. Keep your promise. Many people have told me countless stories of their parents who never kept their promises. They never forgot nor forgave. A cautionary guideline: Decide between you and your partner who gives permission to the children. They have a way of manipulating their parents when they least expect it.

4. Spend quality time with your children

Do things together. These include reading, taking walks, playing games, and doing house chores together. What children want most is your attention. Bad behaviour is often an attempt to get your attention. Schedule family activities and be sure they include the father, so both parents may have a positive effect on the children. Wives often complain that their husbands do not care about the children and do not spend time with them. Remember that you are the home director, so create programmes that include your husband.

5. Be examples and role models to your children

No amount of correction or discipline can replace parental example or role modelling. Parents must be good role models to their children because children are natural imitators. Deuteronomy 6:5-7 says, "Love the Lord your God with all your heart and with all your soul and with all your strength. These commandments that I give you today are to be upon your hearts. Impress them on your children. Talk about them when you sit at home and when you walk along the road, when you lie down and when you get up."

If parents themselves do not live what they teach their children, the children will realise their hypocrisy and not obey them. They will very likely choose to go in the opposite direction. You must put God's word first and walk in love with your children, if you are to succeed as a parent. Give them time and attention.

You should not yell at your children or provoke them to anger. Parents' words are extremely important. Encourage and praise them. Tell them you love them. Ephesians 6:4 says, "Fathers, do not exasperate your children; instead, bring them up in the training and instruction of the Lord."

Help, My Baby Is Not Well

Illnesses are always a part of the landscape as you raise your children, so choose a good paediatrician for them, whenever they do not feel well. It is best to select one before the babies are born, so that she or he may be available during the deliveries. Ask your general doctor or another mother for a recommendation.

Children often need to see the doctor, when they are young. A good paediatrician does more than just treat illness. She or he helps you develop a comfortable style of parenting, which allows you and your husband to gain confidence in yourselves as parents.

When we were young parents, Bob and I often visited the doctor with our children over their colds, coughs, or poor appetite. Another day it would be because they have not yet started to sit down properly or walk. The doctor was always a great source of encouragement to us. Without him, we could have died of worry.

The sleepless nights after children are born can be a challenge. Be encouraged, though; they do not last forever. In time, you start enjoying them. Children usually settle down by the second month. At four months, they should have settled down sufficiently to allow you to take pleasure in them better. By this time, they would have already established a regular sleeping and feeding cycle and shown endless interest in the environment. At this stage, they gain confidence in their caregivers and appreciate the parents. This is usually a good time to begin training them.

Children and Goal Setting

A goal is something we want to achieve. It can be big or small, significant or insignificant. It can be immediate, short-term, or long-term. A goal is focused and has a realistic period and a reasonable outcome. Goals should be set in the following areas: physical, spiritual, mental, social, recreational, family, financial, and others as desired.

Goal setting is not a one-time event; it is an ongoing discipline, which changes with time and seasons. It should not be considered an activity that only adults engage in. Just as parents set goals, so too should children, with their parents' help.

Parents should encourage children to set goals for themselves for the following reasons:

1. Become result-oriented.
2. Have a proper direction in life.
3. Learn to be more proactive.
4. Direct energies towards specific directions.
5. Grow to be better organised.
6. Gain respect from peers and become role models to others.
7. Develop into disciplined individuals.

Parents should encourage children to set goals for themselves...

How to set and achieve a goal is one of the most important things your children can learn for their personal, academic, and spiritual life. It is a great discipline, which helps mould your children into becoming dynamic leaders tomorrow.

In management, we learn the importance of setting **SMART** goals, which stand for:

S - Specific
M - Measurable
A - Achievable
R - Realistic
T - Time-framed

SMART goals are as important to children as they are to adults. Goals help your children set and achieve objectives at home and at school. They help build their confidence, especially when they are realised. Goal setting excites me because I am a beneficiary of the practice. My children have also gained from the same.

To help your children, regardless of age, assist them in coming up with goals. It then becomes their—not their teachers'—responsibility to push them towards attaining them. As a mother, I needed to walk the journey with my own children, in every way. Here are some steps to make sure that your children reach their goals.

1. Identify the goal

In order to help your child identify short- and long-term goals effectively, derive them from their list of wishes, wants, desires, and even fantasies. Short-term goals may be as simple as "to finish my homework daily" or "to avoid junk food". A long-term goal might be "to improve memory capacities". The children's ages, maturity levels, degrees of disciplines, commitments, and goodwill determine the appropriate length of time.

2. Develop goal plans

Help your children develop a plan in order to achieve their goals. Encourage them to write down their goals in a special notebook. They need to note both the goal and the steps to follow for realising the goal. For example:

Goal: To obtain a distinction in mathematics at the end of the term and to improve from the usual pass.

How: I will spend an extra hour every day on studying mathematics. I will cut down on my phone time. I will not receive calls or make any calls during the week, only during weekends. I will limit my TV viewing and spend time improving skills.

Ensure that the period is realistic for the children. Adjust their goals, if necessary, instead of pressuring them to stick to the initial plan. It may just cause pressure and tension, and force them to give up. It is also helpful to review their goals periodically, providing them necessary guidelines.

The Goals of Parenting

Parenting can sometimes be portrayed as a burden, but it is a great gift that brings fulfilment in parents' lives. So what do you consider is your goal as a parent? Malachi 2:15 tells us that God seeks godly offspring. On the other hand, Joshua 24:15 records Joshua's oath: "But as for me and my household, we will serve the Lord." How about yours?

It is every parent's desire for their children to grow in stature, knowledge, wisdom, and favour with man and with God, especially the latter. Jesus definitely grew up this way, as documented in Luke 2:40: "And [Jesus] grew and became strong; he was filled with wisdom, and the grace of God was on Him." It is repeated in Luke 2:52, which says, "And Jesus grew in wisdom and stature, and in favour with God and man".

1. Grow in wisdom

What to do to achieve this:

- Recognise that you are responsible for raising your children properly.

- Take an active role in parenting your children. Parents often leave their responsibilities to teachers, caregivers, and relatives, while they pursue other interests.

- Acknowledge that caring for your children must be your goal, whether the children were planned or not and regardless of your preferred gender for them.

- Know that God holds you responsible for raising children. Titus 2:4 states that younger women should be taught to love their children. Love requires caring for them.

In Ephesians 6:4, fathers are commanded to bring up their children in the training and instruction of the Lord. They cannot leave this to others, including their wives. In Genesis 18:19, God chose Abraham to command his children to keep the way of the Lord. In 1 Samuel 3:12-14, God held Eli accountable for the corruption of his sons—not the schools, government, or even Eli's wife. Read these scriptures to your husband so that he knows what the Lord says about his role in parenting.

Parents must accept the goal of raising their children properly and diligently work towards it. They must not leave it to others. As 1 Timothy 5:8 says that if one neglects to provide for his own, especially his immediate household, he has denied the faith and is worse than an unbeliever. (See also Matthew 7:9-11.) As Christians, we should provide wholesome benefits to our children. Meeting their physical needs means providing them with the following:

- A good education
- Preparation for life
- Recreation, entertainment, and enjoyment
- Assistance in planning
- Prayers, and
- Measures to deal with harmful influences, e.g., peers, music, movies, etc, in their lives.

2. Grow in stature

Psychoanalyst Eric Erikson describes the physical, emotional, and psychological stages of development. For example, if your infants' physical and emotional needs are met sufficiently, they complete their task: Develop the ability to trust others. People stymied in the mastery of a task may still move on to the next stage, but they carry with them the remnants of the unfinished task. For instance, if toddlers are not allowed to learn by doing, they develop a sense of doubt in their abilities, which may complicate later attempts at independence. Similarly, preschoolers made to feel that the activities they initiate are bad may develop a sense of guilt, which inhibits them later in life. Details of his theory are discussed below:

Δ. Infant (Trust vs Mistrust), 0 to 18 months

This is also called the Oral Sensory Stage. At this stage of oral gratification, babies put everything in their mouths. Their mothers' visual contact and touch is important in ensuring trust. When babies successfully pass through this stage in life, they learn to trust that life is okay. They have basic confidence in the future. If they fail to experience trust and are constantly frustrated because of their unmet needs, then mistrust occurs. They need maximum comfort with minimal uncertainty to trust themselves, others, and the environment.

Incidentally, many studies of suicides and suicide attempts point to the importance of early years in developing basic beliefs, such as "the world is trustworthy" and "every individual has a right to be here". Not surprisingly, the most significant relationship is with the mother or the most significant and constant caregiver.

B. *Toddler* (Autonomy vs Shame and Doubt), *18 months to 3 years*

During this stage, the children learn to master skills for themselves. Not only do they learn to walk, talk, and feed themselves, they also learn finer motor development and toilet training. They have the opportunity to build self-esteem and autonomy as they gain more control over their bodies and acquire new skills. They are trained to know right from wrong. One of our skills during the "terrible twos" is the ability to use the powerful word "NO".

At this stage, however, children can be very vulnerable, if they are shamed in the process of toilet training or in learning other important skills. If they feel great shame, then they doubt their capacities and suffer low self-esteem. Their most significant relationship is with their parents.

C. *Preschooler* (Initiative vs Guilt), *3 to 5 years*

During this stage, children experience a desire to copy adults around them. They create and initiate play situations. It is a time to explore the world around them and ask the question, "WHY?" Children begin to develop conscience and sexual identity. At this stage, they are usually involved in the classic Oedipal struggle and resolve it through "social role identification". According to Erikson's psychosocial theory, this stage is of unconscious sexual desires, especially for the male child, for the parent of the opposite sex, usually accompanied by hostility to the parent of the same sex. If they are frustrated over natural desires and goals, they may easily experience guilt.

D. School-Age Child (Industry vs Inferiority), 6 to 12 years

This stage is often referred to as the Latency Stage. Children become capable of learning, creating, and accomplishing numerous new skills and knowledge; they thus develop a sense of industry. This is also a very social stage of development. If they experience unresolved feelings of inadequacy and inferiority among their peers, then they can have serious problems in terms of competence and self-esteem. The children try to develop a sense of self-worth by refining skills.

E. Adolescent (Identity vs Role Confusion), 12 to 19 years

At this stage, identity is important and the children—now adolescents—learn how to answer the question, "Who am I?" satisfactorily and happily. Even the best-adjusted adolescents experience some role identity diffusion, though. Rebellion flourishes at this time; self-doubt floods the youngsters' minds, and so on. Parents are unable to identify with them. Everything about them changes to the surprise of their parents. If the parents do not understand this stage, they could lose their children, being unable to control them.

Erikson believes that during successful early adolescence, mature time perspective is developed. Adolescents acquires self-certainty as opposed to self-consciousness and self-doubt. They have the capacity and they experiment with different, usually constructive roles rather than adopt a negative identity such as delinquency. They actually anticipate achievement and go for it rather than be controlled by feelings of fear and inferiority or by an inadequate time perspective. In later adolescence, clear sexual identity (manhood or womanhood) is established. At this point, it is important that parents take time to explain sex and sexuality and expected behaviour, in order to avoid disappointments. Adolescents seek leadership, longing for someone to inspire them. They want to be understood and gradually develop a set of ideals, which is socially congruent and desirable, in the case of successful adolescents. Role models are key in the life of young persons at this stage.

F. *Young Adult (Intimacy vs Isolation), 18 to 35 years*

At the young adult stage, people seek companionship and security of love with significant others other than family. Some also begin to to narrow down in relationships, get married, and start their families. Young adults seek deep intimacy and satisfying relationships. If unsuccessful, isolation may occur. At this stage, significant relationships are with marital partners and friends.

Finally, adolescents grow into young adults. For the first time, successful young adults can experience true intimacy— the sort that makes good marriages possible or genuine friendships endure.

These development stages help parents understand their children and deal with their particular needs and challenges along the journey of life.

3. Have favour with man and with God

"Favour" means to give special regard or to treat with goodwill, to show exceptional kindness to someone. Sometimes, it means to show extra kindness in treating others, that is, to show preferential treatment. This is the favour from God: He treats us much better than we deserve. We must understand God's favour in degrees. Here are some ways by which we obtain the Lord's favour:

- Praying to the Lord (Job 33:26)

- Keeping the Lord's commandments (Proverbs 3:1-4)

- Seeking and finding God's wisdom (Proverbs 8:35)

- Searching for and doing good (Proverbs 11:27, 12:2)

- Living righteously (Proverbs 14:9)

My father always reminded me that there are things money cannot buy: One of them is favour, and the other is one's reputation. Proverbs is quick to confirm that a good name is more desirable than great riches and favour is better than silver and gold (Proverbs 22:1). God can choose to give you favour. When He does, wonderful things can happen, which leave no doubt in your mind that you are loved and highly favoured by Him.

Favour takes you where nothing else can take you. It can open doors of opportunity that you cannot begin to think or even imagine. In Genesis 26:24, God appeared to Isaac and said, "I am the God of your father Abraham. Do not be afraid, for I am with you; I will bless you and will increase the number of your descendants for the sake of my servant Abraham." Favour is our inheritance as descendants of Abraham. God has promised to bless you; His favour is upon you. Simply acknowledge and call upon Him to reign in your life. The Lord's promises are true!

Here are some Bible verses to ponder and meditate on:

My son, do not forget my teaching, but keep my commands in your heart, for they will prolong your life many years and bring you peace and prosperity. Let love and faithfulness never leave you; bind them around your neck, write them on the tablet of your heart. Then you will win favour and a good name in the sight of God and man. Trust in the Lord with all your heart and lean not on your own understanding... (Proverbs 3:1-5)

Blessed are those who listen to me, watching daily at my doors, waiting at my doorway. For those who find me find life and receive favour from the Lord. (Proverbs 8:34-35)

Chapter Nine

Coping With the Other Woman in His Life

Many women do noble things,
but you surpass them all.
Proverbs 31:29

A s all married couples find out eventually, marriage involves more people than just a man and a woman committed to live the rest of their lives together. The relationship opens the door to a new set of relatives and friends. These people have tremendous influence on them.

When I got married, one of my mother's concerns was how I was to fit into a big, polygamous family, since I was brought up in a tight, monogamous home. At that time, I did not see what all the fuss was about. What did the entire clan have to do with my marriage? After all, I was marrying my sweetheart, not the entire family. However, it did not take long before I got the answer to my question. I soon realised that by marrying their son, I had become the newest member of my husband's family. I now had a duty to learn their culture and to develop good, healthy relationships with each individual in the family, if I was to enjoy my marriage.

Of course, knowledge of my responsibilities and their actual execution were two different things. I had already won the trust and confidence of the man in my life but not that of his mother, sisters, brothers, and extended family. I made my mistakes, but as I appreciated the importance of the various relationships, I put in the necessary effort and worked on them tirelessly. While various

Relationships with mothers-in-law can be one of the greatest challenges in a marriage.

family relationships undoubtedly have tremendous influence on the marriage, I wish to focus on the one dreaded by most brides: their relationship with their mothers-in-law.

Like every woman, I had opportunities to hear many horror stories about mothers-in-law. Thankfully, I had none of my own; I love my husband's mother. She gives me space to be myself. She is kind, considerate, and humble. I know many of you have or will have one just like mine, but I am also aware that many have relationships with mothers-in-law that have never worked.

In most women's meetings I attend, the topic of mothers-in-law never fails to come up. In a bridal shower I facilitated, a young woman came up to me even before the end of the session to say, "My mother-in-law thinks my husband is her personal belonging, her handyman. She makes all the decisions for us and criticises me at every possible opportunity. I have never gotten over the fact that she told me, during our wedding, that she had preferred someone else over me. It has been 15 years since and we have never hit it off. We continue to be rivals despite my efforts."

Relationships with mothers-in-law can be one of the greatest challenges in a marriage. More often than not, a small misunderstanding can cause the marriage to suffer tension. This often triggers a ripple effect that affects your relationships with your husband and in-laws. Taken for granted, the ripple effect can seriously damage the marital relationship.

The following are some of the complaints raised against mothers-in-law:

- She never leaves us alone.
- She keeps meddling into our affairs.
- She always tells me what to do.
- She wants constant companionship.
- She competes with me for my husband's attention.
- She never admits her mistakes.
- She has no respect for me.

I am sure you may have one or two to add to this list.

Whether these complaints are true or not, it is important to nurture an acceptable and cordial relationship with the mother of your husband. Instead of concentrating on perceived wrongs, you can take steps to make the relationship better. Let me share some helpful thoughts.

Hit the Ground Running

It is crucial that your relationship with your mother-in-law starts on a good and positive note. Always remember that she is the vessel God used to bring forth your beloved husband. For that alone, you owe her much. She brought him up well to become the fine young man who blesses your life so much. You may think her irrelevant and that she has little to do with your husband's development. The truth, however, is that what he is today is because of her. Regardless of your judgement, know that she had remarkable influence over him and his present characteristics. Of course, this is not always the case or the ideal situation. Your spouse may not have had the privilege of being brought up by his biological mother or may have had one who was cruel, which strained their relationship. Regardless of the circumstances, you need to build a healthy relationship with her. She is the bloodline of your children.

Most differences develop in the run-up to the wedding, especially during the preparations and associated ceremonies. To start your relationship right, make your mother-in-law feel part of the wedding arrangements. Seek her opinion on key issues, even if you already know what you want to do. Make her feel valued.

I have often heard young people say, "It is my wedding!" There is no dispute that it is "your" wedding and that it is an important stage in your life; however, it is also an important stage in "her" life. The baby she nurtured, developed, and empowered is about to leave her to begin a journey she cannot control. That alone causes her feelings of uncertainty and anxiety. This is a very difficult situation for her and your understanding and cooperation is helpful.

Know That It Is Not a Contest

Before you came along, there was a woman in your man's life called Mum. She carried him in her womb for nine months, gave birth to him with some measure of pain, nurtured him, educated him, corrected him, and so forth. As he grew up, he needed Mum's approval before he could do this or that. Only later did he become an independent man, ready to start his life with another woman: you.

I do not say this to belittle your place in his life. I only seek to remind you that Mum is important and has played a major role in your man's life. For that reason, she should still have a place in his life. Upon marriage, though, her role changes. Although she has given up her spot in his life so you can take centre stage, she is still relevant. Whether or not she played her part perfectly does not change the fact that she is Mum.

Note that men love their mothers—at least most of them do. I am not sure if it has anything to do with the contentious Oedipus complex theorised by Sigmund Freud. Freud puts the Oedipal stage at between three to five years. It is a stage where children experience an erotic attachment to the parent of the opposite sex and hostility toward the same-sex parent. In his opinion, a boy is fixated on his mother and competes with his father for her attention. The opposite is the attraction of a girl to her father and rivalry with her mother, which he calls the Electra complex.

In addition, during female psychosexual development, a young girl is initially attached to her mother. When she discovers that she does not have a penis, she becomes attached to her father and begins to resent her mother who she blames for her "castration". As a result, Freud believed that the girl then begins to identify with and emulate her mother out of fear of losing her love. Whilst children's understanding of the full sexual act may be questioned, they do feel some kind of primitive, physical sensations for their parents. Whether the theory holds water or not, one thing is certain: Boys love their mothers.

If you want to lose the admiration and respect of your man, criticise his mother. Many women fail to get along well with their mothers-in-law because they feel a constant need to compete with them for their man's affection and attention. Encourage your man to eliminate the need for a competitive relationship by making it clear to his mother what her new role is. He can eliminate the competition by clarifying to everyone that you are the most important woman in his life. You are not in a popularity contest, but there is always room for both you and your mother-in-law. Both of you love the same man, so get along for his sake, the children's, and that of the rest of his family. My son's wife, in sensing my apprehension during their marriage, said to me: "Mum, relax. Your son has a big heart and has a place for both of us."

I was so glad that she said that. Just hearing that meant so much to me. I certainly did not want to be deserted just because he had found the love of his life. I did recognise, though, that my dominant role in his life was over. I rejoiced with him that he had found the one he loves.

Acknowledge Your Differences

God created us all differently; no two people are quite alike. We can respond to these differences by constantly fighting or by celebrating our diversity. Each of you have different expectations as far as your relationship is concerned. Your mother-in-law may want you to be the daughter she never had, but you feel smothered by her constant visits and/or involvement in your life. Or the opposite may be true and you may want to have a closer relationship with her than she wants with you.

I am reminded of many people who have lived through this. For some, the mother-in-law is so aloof, she does not play any role in the children's or grandchildren's lives. For others, she may want to visit them more often than they like. Just because you have different expectations does not mean either of you is wrong. Try to find a common ground. I assure you: Nothing is impossible with the Lord. If anyone is to change, it should be you because you are responsible for what you choose. You cannot take charge of or control the choices other people make.

Be Assertive and Set Your Boundaries

All relationships require boundaries of one kind or another. Your relationship with your mother-in-law should not be any different. Boundaries protect one from being invaded within their territories. You are a confident young woman, so behave like one. As long as you know what you want and how you want it, other people will respect you for it. If you do not like unexpected visits from your mother-in-law, have a structured visitation that both of you are comfortable with.

Whatever the issues are, remember that it is not necessary to involve third parties, unless it is critical. Develop your own communication channels that will be efficient, effective, and friendly. Treat your mother-in-law the way you want your husband or your brother's wife to treat your mother. If your husband wants to draw a boundary concerning your own mother, how would you want him to treat her? Would you want him to be arrogant and insulting? Or would you want him to be respectful and mature? If you treat your husband's mother the way you want him to treat yours, then you have the added bonus of gaining his respect.

Accord Her the Respect She Deserves

Your mother-in-law is an older woman, with lots of life experience. Although you may not always agree with her, show her the respect she deserves. She can have a lot of influence on your life through your spouse, so give her a deserved place on the throne. She can also be a source of blessing to you and your children and generations thereafter.

Be Helpful

Your mother-in-law appreciates a good work ethic, no matter the task. By being helpful, you prove yourself a good person to her. Offer to help her with little things that are important to her. Plan visits to her home, without necessarily involving your husband. After all, girls need their time together. Bond with her as much as possible; that is up to you to do. As much as he loves you, he cannot help you bond with his mother. Your generous attitude leaves your mother-in-law proud to be in your company.

Communicate Often

Communicate, communicate, and communicate. It is a big part of a good relationship with your mother-in-law. The bond between you and her needs to be based on mutual respect, understanding, and trust. It takes some time, effort, and hard work, but it will turn out to be a worthy investment in the end.

The complaint of many mothers-in-law is "being left out". Consistent communication goes a long way in making her feel included and loved. It helps to let her know of major decisions or events in good time, so she does not find out through other people first. This can offend her and cost you her trust. A popular Kikuyu proverb says, "*Ndûgû Nî Makinya*". (Friendship is nurtured through regular visits.)

How often do you talk to your mother-in-law? It is important to allow her into your life, if you want your relationship with her to grow. Tell her even about your trivial things and make her feel a part of your immediate family. Go the extra mile and find out what she likes; go out of your way to please her just to get into her good books. Your mother-in-law is as important as your biological mother; if you call your mother often, why not call your mother-in-law just to check on her and find out how she is?

If you marry someone from a different tribe, you may need to learn his language. This helps you communicate easily with his "people". We go out of our way to learn languages like Chinese, French, and Japanese, yet we find it difficult to learn our spouse's language. I know of a Kikuyu woman who married a Luo man and moved to his rural home. If you were to meet her today, you would confuse her for a Luo. She speaks, behaves, and interacts with her rural folks just like one of them. This is the way to behave. If you love your spouse, you should also love his people. You are married to him, but if you do not love his people as well, you can have a very unhappy marriage.

Be Her Jewel and Crown

If you want to have a good relationship with your mother-in-law, you need to be a person that she can want to have a relationship with. You need to be a good person in your daily life, so she can be proud to have you as a daughter-in-law. Be the Proverbs 31 woman, who leads her home with integrity, influence, diligence, discipline, compassion, and giftedness.

Cherish Her Son

If you think about it, your mother-in-law has raised your spouse from day one. No wonder she struggles with the idea of her child living with you! Part of a good relationship with your mother-in-law is to give her the peace of mind that her child is loved, appreciated, and cared for. I often speak to my daughter-in-law, my son's wife. I thank her simply for loving my son and making him happy. Your mother-in-law will be much more pleasant and approachable, if she knows you make her son happy.

Chapter Ten

Marriage and friendship

Friendship is there wherever you go
Friendship is there when you overdose
Friendship loves and Friendship cares
Friendship is life with a little dare
Kelsey Harshaw

As my son made his vows to his beloved bride on their wedding day, something he said caught my attention. In his vows, which he had written himself, he declared, "Today, I marry my best friend!" How precious and wonderful that people should marry their best friends.

We may not give it much thought, but friendship between spouses is not only very important, it glues a marriage together. In my experience, the common denominator in most fulfilled, lasting, and happy marriages is the firm foundation of friendship upon which the unions are built. This strong friendship is evident in the beginning of the relationship and throughout the entire marriage journey.

True, lasting friendship in marriage is not built overnight; it takes time. Just as a house is built one brick at a time, so also is the marital relationship built. Friendship and intimacy are built up one thoughtful action at a time, one kind word at a time. The couple must commit themselves to developing high levels of intimacy. This involves becoming familiar with one another: knowing each other's likes, dislikes, ambitions, dreams, personalities, strengths, and weaknesses. When one falls, the other lifts him up. When one is cold, the other warms him up. When one is lonely, the other provides companionship. When one falls apart and is disillusioned, the other lifts him up. Most importantly, learn to trust one another completely. In the absence of trust, friendship is impossible.

As important as friendship is in marriage, I sometimes hear of couples who are afraid of developing too close a bond; they argue that familiarity breeds contempt. I can confidently say that familiarity actually has the capacity to create a bond that goes beyond description. It builds togetherness and establishes a sense of safety and contentment. The relationship grows greatly as a result.

My Husband, My Friend

One of the reasons that I continue to hold on, even when things seem to fall apart is simple: Someone believes in me and cares enough to listen, to hold my hand, and to be there for me, regardless of circumstances. My husband and I have always been best friends. Because of this, we have tended to encourage one another in the path of life and to grow together. Failure to develop and maintain intimacy can be costly as some couples find out. Listen to the following stories of despair:

Brian and Betty have had a largely enjoyable marriage. Lately, however, they have become aware of a growing gap between them, a vacuum that has brought a sense of hollowness with it. According to Betty, their relationship went well, until the children came. The responsibilities that came with them and other influences have caused them to drift apart. Betty often complains that Brian is too preoccupied with his work. In spite of her expressed desire to have more time with him, he is too busy in his pursuit of professional success to be available for her. Betty feels he is insensitive to her needs, causing them to grow apart. Their sex life is a reflection of this apathy, so she feels lonely in the relationship. The emotional distance hurts her very much. She does not know what to do.

On their part, Joyce and John were very close when they dated and spent a lot of time together. Whenever you saw Joyce, you knew John was not far away. We greatly admired their closeness. We aspired for their kind of relationship and romance. They represented what we respected: the rare ideal couple. However, years down the line, it became clear that they had lost the spark. The togetherness and friendship that made them so admirable were no longer evident. The fire of friendship and intimacy that once defined their relationship had turned to cold ashes. The usual suspects were again to blame: a demanding work schedule, children, financial challenges, and friendships. They had taken their toll on the relationship. They each seemed to have developed separate lives.

According to Joyce, it eventually became difficult for the couple to have any meaningful conversation. Although they had talked a lot in the past, they now hardly said anything to each another. In the past, they shared the same circle of friends; now, they socialise alone. They cannot stand each other. They fight over anything and everything. They now pull in different directions and cannot seem to agree on anything! Their precious intimacy is gone.

I wish I could say that these are two isolated cases of intimacy gone bust. These two couples' experiences actually represent the reality of many marriages today. Their separate paths and conflicting choices have caused them to grow in totally different and incompatible directions. They lost the glue that held them together: the bond of friendship. Couples also grow apart as a result of socioeconomic status.

Other friends in Marriage

My dictionary defines a friend as "a close or intimate acquaintance, a well-wisher, or a supporter". We make our friends in school, at our workplaces, or at our churches. As the path of life stretches out, we outgrow some friends and lose contact with others. Some betray us and we become rivals or sworn enemies against them. Eventually, some do turn out to be "friends that stick closer than brothers". They become our spouses. What happens to the rest?

If you marry a friend with whom you share a circle of friends, you retain your friendships after marriage. If you have your own bosom friends whom you would like to keep even afterwards, it is advisable you introduce them to your intended spouse during the dating period. However, be aware that the dynamics of your relationships with them changes when you say "I do", especially if they are of the opposite sex and single.

After you say "I do", your loyalty, priority, and devotion switches to your spouse. Everybody and everything takes a subordinate position. If your spouse does not like or enjoy the company of your friends, consider his views without being defensive. He may want you to get rid of them fast. Maintain distance for a while, negotiate where necessary, and let him know that he is the priority. Your and his priorities are important to you. After all, it is in your and his best interest for the marriage to work. It may be hard, but your submission may save your marriage.

Marriage does establish limits on your involvements with former friends, especially if they are still single. You cannot have your usual girls' nights out without the express consent of your spouse. You certainly look for big trouble, if you insist on keeping close relationships with friends of the opposite sex. You establish a minefield and breeding ground for jealousy and distrust.

This does not, however, mean you cannot have friends or colleagues of the opposite sex with whom you relate with from time to time. If they are worth your time and effort, the courteous thing to do is to introduce them to your spouse. If they are not comfortable with your spouse, that is an alarm bell. The reality of friendships in marriage is that you cannot live as a single person anymore. Two are now one. No individual in the marriage has the sole decision to establish friendships at the expense of the other. You should not have any friends unknown to your spouse, unless you have something to hide.

A more sensitive situation is preserving relationships with ex-boyfriends, ex-lovers, or ex-husbands, especially if a child is involved. The relationship must be clearly defined and boundaries established with the consent of your current spouse. If there is no child or common interests between you and your ex, dissolve the relationships altogether. You must do it, if you want your marriage to be void of suspicions and doubts. Ex-lovers have a way of getting back together with you at the expense of your marriage. Flee every appearance of evil. Be "a woman after God's own heart". Every wise woman builds her house, but the foolish one brings it down with her hands.

Life naturally dictates our friends. You make friends with people you share common interests with. Most likely, you have friends from church, if you attend its activities regularly. The same applies to sports, workplaces, and schools. When you have children, you develop friendships with other parents as well. The same applies to you when you are pregnant. Your single friends gradually become irrelevant. If they do not get married soon, they fade away.

But no matter how many other friends you have, your spouse should be your best friend. You also need to have at least one very close friend of the same sex whom you can talk to and share things with. She should be close enough to tell you the truth and to rebuke you when you err. Your spouse should know who she is, though. Friends like that are rare to find, but when you find them, they are an immense blessing to your home.

friends Turned Strangers

Going back to our friends turned strangers: How did they end up where they are? The reasons can be as diverse as there are couples. Each couple should retrace their steps and see where they lost it. I believe the following observations should serve as an example as you seek your own answers:

Disproportionate Development

While most partners start at the same level, it is common for one partner to rise much faster intellectually, socially, and so on, than the other does. Over the years, they may grow in different directions rather than together. This problem gives rise to a communication breakdown. For couples to grow together, they have to pull one another along the journey of life. After all, what are friends for?

The word "friendship" evokes thoughts of sacrifice, vulnerability, companionship, mutual respect, and a high level of honesty. It implies that we consult one another, do things together, and enjoy each other's company because friends pull in the same direction, without selfish ambition. I know many women who have grown intellectually, leaving their men behind. Individuals do grow at their own pace and set their own goals and ambitions in terms of intellectual growth. It is helpful, however, that as a wife, you keep yourself abreast with your husband's world.

It is not possible for a marriage to last, while you are not on the same intellectual levels. It is good to belong to your partner's world by understanding him. Have informed and intelligent discussions on things that pertain to work, politics, and life in general.

Rival Opinions

Friends do not always have to agree on everything. It is normal for them to have differing opinions and views on certain things and still respect one another's views. Remember that men and women are wired differently, so it is fine to see things that way as well. Disagreements are part of marriage; there is no time that you live free from them, but it does not mean that you cannot compromise on issues.

Reigniting the Friendship

Whatever your reason for drifting apart, all is not lost. If you have lost the glue, it is not too late to reignite the friendship with your partner. If you have already lost the friendship with your partner, do not be afraid; it can be restored. Plan to have common ground—something that you and your partner enjoy doing together, in order to find a new beginning. Your marriage can be stronger, if you can do some things together. New memories and each other's company are means of nourishing your marriage to make it last! God is faithful to give us new beginnings, so you can have it now by making an effort to rebuild the friendship.

However, you have to brace yourself for a great deal of work and much sacrifice and perseverance, not to mention faith and lots of prayer. After all, God promises to grant us the desires of our heart. The following steps should be of great help:

Christ First

Christ first is the secret to building a lasting relationship with your spouse. As the Bible reminds us, "Unless the Lord builds the house, the builders labour in vain" (Psalm 127:1). Hearts filled with Christ's love can never be very far apart. With Christ in the home, marriage can be successful. The gospels are the cure for all marriages filled with hatred, bitterness, and disappointment. It prevents thousands of divorces by miraculously restoring love and happiness.

Preparedness to Work

Relationships do not just happen; they are initiated, worked on, and nurtured. You can only reap the benefits of what you sow. Friendship has to be cared for on a daily basis, if it is to continue. Your responsibility is to do your part and leave your partner to do his. If they do not respond or do what they should, it does not mean that you withdraw your friendship. Patience pays, and what you sow, you reap in good time.

If partners do not give enough attention to developing and growing the friendship, then things fall apart, opening doors for boredom, infidelity, failure, and many enemies. Friendship is the foundation of a happy, lasting marriage. It is so important in the marriage relationship because it includes other essential areas of the relationship. Friends do everything together, including romance and great sex.

Preparedness to Embrace Change

A marriage should never be based on the assumption that nothing changes. Everything does, including your own looks, your lifestyle, your friends, and even your outlook in life. Once the children arrive, they change your life even more, when they grow up.

The most important thing for a marriage to last is not to lose sight of the essentials. Many things come and go, but the things that should never change are your values and beliefs, and your respect for your spouse. Erotic energies and romance alone cannot hold a marriage together, but values can.

Compromise and Forgiveness

Every marriage needs a good dose of compromise, patience, and tolerance. Forgiveness is crucial in building the marriage relationship. Do not keep a record of wrongs. When dealing with conflict, stick to the issue at hand; do not bring up things of the past.

Your Vows Remembered

What God has joined, let no man separate! Always remember your marriage vows. You are united as one in marriage. Ideally, you should be together forever. Love each other and be faithful, so you can make the marriage last forever.

Prayer

Consider the following scriptures that talk about prayer:

- "Watch and pray so that you will not fall into temptation. The spirit is willing, but the flesh is weak." (Matthew 26:41)

- "...[P]ray for each other..." (James 5:16)

- "If any of you lacks wisdom, you should ask God, who gives generously to all without finding fault, and it will be given to you." (James 1:5)

Praying together is the most powerful tool in our marriage relationship. It has a way of dissolving heartaches and making everything simply beautiful. Pray aloud for each other! This wonderful experience succeeds beyond our wildest dreams. Ask God for forgiveness, strength, wisdom, solutions to problems, His protection, and His provision.

The praying person is not automatically cured of all of her faults, but she has a heart that wants to do right. This keeps the family intact. There is a popular plaque in most houses that reads, "A family that prays together, stays together". I encourage you to learn the practice of prayer because it is an awesome gift!

When all is said and done, the wife that wants her marriage to work must think and approach her marriage as a farmer approaches his farm. A good farmer knows that no matter how good his intentions or skills are, there are factors that can make all his hard work amount to nothing. Let us look at them one at a time and connect them to the marriage experience.

1. A good farmer first identifies good soil for his seed

Your good intentions for a good marriage alone cannot guarantee one because it is about two people. You cannot marry the wrong person and assume that your good seed and hard work gives you a good marriage. If the soil is bad, it does not matter what else you do. Go back to Chapter One again and review my thoughts on what constitutes a suitable mate.

2. A good farmer prepares the ground

Good ground must be prepared to receive the seed. Just because you have met the right person does not mean you are ready to start a home together. There are always "bushes" to be cleared, "stumps" to be uprooted, and "hard soil" to be broken. Courtship is not just a time to feel good; it is time to deal with issues that hinder the union.

3. A good farmer plants good seed

What you plant is what you ultimately harvest. If you plant good thoughts in your partner, it is what you reap. If you plant bitterness, anger, distrust, selfishness, jealousy, and other negative emotions in your marriage, then you reap a negative outcome. If you plant love, commitment, and selflessness, you reap love and security.

4. A good farmer tends his plants

Commit yourself to water and tend the things you plant in your marriage. There are always "weeds", which seek to compete with what you have planted. Remove them continually and water the plants with consistent love and devotion. Water your marriage with ceaseless prayer.

5. A good farmer, having done what he needs to do, trusts God to bring him a good harvest

Finally, know that you can only go so far. Having done what you need to do, allow God to do what only He can do. Refuse to manipulate things to work out how and when you want them to do so. Learn to trust that He who brought you together has a good plan for you and brings it to pass in due course.

Bibliography

Chapman, Gary. *The Five Love Languages: How to Express Heartfelt Commitment to Your Mate.* New South Wales: Strand Publishing, 1992.

Erikson, Eric. *Childhood and Society,* 2nd ed. New York: Aronson, 1963.

Firestone, Robert, and Joyce Catlett. *Fear of Intimacy.* Washington, DC: American Psychological Association, 1999.

Freud, Sigmund. *Theory of Human Development.* New York: Norton, 1949.

Gray, John. *Men Are from Mars, Women Are from Venus: Practical Guide for Improving Communication and Getting What You Want in Your Relationships.* New York: HarperCollins, 1998.

Harley, Willard. *His Needs, Her Needs: Building an Affair-Proof Marriage.* Grand Rapids: Fleming H Revell, 1986.

Hauck, Paul. *How to Bring Up Your Child Successfully.* London: Sheldon, 1982.

Hendrix, Harville. *Getting the Love You Want: A Guide for Couples.* New York: Holt Paperbacks, 2008.

Lee, Nicky and Sila. *The Marriage Book: How to Build a Lasting Relationship.* London: Alpha International, 2000.

Maxwell, John. *The Winning Attitude: Your Pathway to Personal Success.* Nashville: Thomas Nelson, 1993.

Olson, David, and Amy Olson. *Empowering Couples: Building on Your Strengths.* Minneapolis: Life Innovations, 2000.

Ornish, Dean. *Love and Survival: The Scientific Basis for the Healing Power of Intimacy.* New York: HarperCollins, 1998.

Peck, M. Scott. *The Road Less Travelled: A New Psychology of Love, Traditional Values, and Spiritual Growth.* New York: Simon & Schuster, 1978.

Rogers, Carl. *On Becoming a Person: A Therapist's View of Psychotherapy.* New York: Houghton Mifflin, 1989.

Schaefer, Mark, and David Olson. *"Assessing Intimacy: The PAIR inventory."* Journal of Marital and Family Therapy 7 (1981): 47-60.

Stahmann, Robert, Wayne Young, and Julie Grover. *Becoming One: Intimacy in Marriage.* American Fork: Covenant Communications, 2004.

Stanley, Scott, Daniel Trathen, Savanna McCain, and Milt Bryan. *A Lasting Promise: A Christian Guide to Fighting for Your Marriage.* San Francisco: Jossey-Bass, 1998.

Stanley, Thomas, and William Danko. *The Millionaire Next Door.* New York: Pocket Books, 1996.

Tongoi, Dennis. *Mixing God with Money: Strategies for Living in an Uncertain Economy.* Nairobi: Bezalel Investments, 2004.

Wheat, Ed. *Love Life for Every Married Couple.* Grand Rapids: Zondervan, 1980.

Williamson, Marianne. *A Return to Love: Reflections on the Principles of a Course in Miracles.* London: HarperCollins, 1992.

The author would appreciate your feedback through

http://marriagebuilttolast.wordpress.com

jennie@karina.co.ke

www.jenniekarina.co.ke